THE ETIQUETTE

of

LEADERSHIP

The Art and Science of Leading Well

BEN BALDWIN ＊ **IAN SAMPSON**

THE ETIQUETTE OF LEADERSHIP
The Art and Science of Leading Well

For general information on our other products and services, please find our contact information online at www.theleadershipfoundation.com.au

To purchase customized or bulk copies of this book, please visit us online at

www.theleadershipfoundation.com.au

The Leadership Foundation assists developing and accomplished leaders to discover and build their unique leadership identity. Members are enabled to reflect and plan their leadership journey in all areas of their personal and work life. The Leadership Foundation runs public and in-house programs based on exploration through conversation and personal reflection. The Foundation also hosts a series of lunches in Brisbane Australia where new and experienced leaders build connections, gain mentoring and explore important leadership issues that build confidence and mastery. Our aim is to help you create leadership worthy of being followed.

CONTENTS

INTRODUCTION

Leadership is an industry. If you Google the word "leadership" you will get hundreds upon millions of hits. More management books are written on leadership than any other topic. Every day hundreds of articles appear in newspapers, blogs and discussion groups about aspects of leadership. No doubt they all make a contribution to the avid reader's education—but do they actually contribute to the practice of real leadership?

Much of the writing, conferences, and workshops involves talk *about* leadership, much like a commentator describes a new car, the wedding of a couple or an artistic performance. But writing *about* these things is not the same as experiencing the actual thrill of a new car, the romance of a wedding or the movement of the soul that occurs in a performance. For all the descriptions about leadership, something is often left unsaid. There is usually an unspoken dimension that those seeking to build their leadership capacity can't quite access. It can be like looking at a jigsaw that is complete except for just one piece; somehow the picture doesn't translate fully until that last piece goes into place.

This book is designed to provide what is missing; to provide full access and complete the jigsaw. It does this by uncovering the principles and practical approaches, what some would call *manners*, that good leaders almost always use. When they are uncovered, you will be able to understand what it is that you are seeing when a good leader moves others to action. You will be able to identify, through reflection and practice, the unique ways that your manners can help you be an effective or efficient leader. It provides practical ways for you to realize your own leadership potential. You will also be able to build the effectiveness of your leadership performance.

The Etiquette of Leadership is a body of practical knowledge that can show you the way of leadership. It is not a collection of theories. It is not a new theory. It seeks to draw on time-honored understandings that have developed over hundreds of years, in every facet of life where leadership is exercised effectively. From that basis, we seek to build insights and understandings that you can apply in your daily guidance, creatively and innovatively. Equipped with a good knowledge of the Etiquette of Leadership, every leadership statement you make and action you conduct will build on your unique understanding and the ways you apply that, to provide new methods for interactions in the moment to occur.

We want to make it very clear at the start of this work that the Etiquette of Leadership is inclusive; it is not religious, nor discriminatory towards any others on the basis of a characteristic they have. It can be practiced by leaders of any kind towards others of any kind without regard to divisions based on sex, color, religion, beliefs, practices, societal standing, etc.

Just as The Etiquette of Leadership is neither a collection of theories nor a new approach, there are other things that the Etiquette of Leadership is not about. It is not about traditional *etiquette* based on the historical myths and legends of chivalry and associated notions of a so-called Golden Age; an age that never actually existed apart from what was in the minds of poets and romantic novelists.

The Etiquette of Leadership is also not about elitism. It does not set out to create physical or social divisions between people or to create the basis of judgments about others. It does not presume to create a notion that those who practice the Etiquette of Leadership are in any way better, worthier, more noble, more knowing, of a higher class or character than others. The Etiquette of Leadership is inclusive, not exclusive. When practiced well, the Etiquette of Leadership allows for elegance, grace, and understanding to emerge from the leader's words and actions and to create liveliness for the follower.

The third thing that the Etiquette of Leadership is not about is a particular style, theory or type of leadership. Because some readers will have distinct notions of the meaning of the term *The Etiquette of Leadership* that are drawn from common *etiquette* we want to mention just one style of leadership as an example.

Much of the literature on leadership concerns the heroism of leadership; the idea of delivering a heartfelt speech to the troops and then leading them over the top of the trenches and into battle, possibly never to return. The Etiquette of Leadership is not a matter of life and death; it is much more important than that! It is about the miracles of life-giving, life-sustaining and life-empowering leadership that occur every day through your exercise of the Etiquette of Leadership.

The Etiquette of Leadership is life-creating, in the moment, every day. It is an important part of what sustains life. An example in work situations is the leader who acts with the Etiquette of Leadership and keeps the system functioning efficiently, sustainably and enables those around them. But for their leadership, the system would do what all systems are naturally inclined to do—experience entropy and decline. But for their efficient and sustainable leadership, people would experience ineffectiveness and all the things that flow from that: dissatisfaction, disaffection, disengagement, disjointedness, disempowerment, dismissal, disablement, disability, etc. However, for all this it would be a caricature of the Etiquette of Leadership to describe it as just another form of heroic leadership or that heroic leadership is a form of the kind of leadership we are calling forth here. Heroic leadership may become part of your unique Etiquette of Leadership. It is for you to decide or not.

The Etiquette of Leadership always seeks to encourage those who practice it efficiently to create outcomes that could not have otherwise have been achieved in a situation, circumstance, chapter, event, stage or another time-bound element of life.

This book has been written with two outcomes in mind: to help you be a truly effective leader and to help you be at ease with your own uniqueness as a leader. We start from the premise that you already have thoughts, ideas, theories and practical experience, at least to some degree, about leadership. Whether you are a new leader or a veteran, this book is intended to be a hands-on guide that you can use every day to build your leadership capability and effectiveness. There are some insights you will use immediately; others you will want to reflect on, practice and build your prowess more gradually.

Work out your own Etiquette of Leadership. Use this material to guide you in developing your own approach, your own protocol that works for you. The test is whether it works for you and those you seek to lead. The result is that, if they follow you, you will create what you strive to create.

Every leader develops their own Etiquette of Leadership. What we are trying to do is to make it visible and explicit, so it can be consciously developed and refined by you, for you.

In this journey, you will notice other leaders' Etiquette of Leadership and be able to assess whether their practices and approaches are working for them, and may or may not be useful for you to adopt or at least consider.

The reason this book is called *The Etiquette of Leadership* and not *Leadership Etiquette* is this: leadership etiquette could be just a list of practical tips and tricks that people in positions of leadership should do. The Etiquette of Leadership is about how leadership that is exercised with highly functional etiquette brings a new dimension to situations. It enlivens the situation and the people in it.

Some years ago, one of us was attending a lecture at a Business School when a guest speaker was introduced who told his story as a Chief Operating Officer (COO) of a large national organization.

He had been in the role for only nine months, but the way that he spoke was inspiring, demonstrating real leadership and showing how noble a leader can be when they are practicing the Etiquette of Leadership—albeit he was unaware at the time that that was what he was doing.

This COO addressed a group of 30 executives and admitted how poorly the industry had been operating, leading to the collapse of the largest single provider within their industry. This resulted in the establishment of their organization and the COO taking ownership of where they had been. He shone a light on the mistakes that had been made, acknowledged them and held himself responsible for correcting past actions. When he spoke of what needed to happen moving forward, he talked in terms of "we." He didn't stand there proclaiming himself as a hero. Instead, he spoke about how he identified that leadership was needed, how he accepted the role but was clear that it would take all the skills, experience and drive of the team to make this organization great. He was sure of himself as a leader; he believed in and had confidence in his followership. It was a short and straightforward talk, but truly amazing.

As you practice the Etiquette of Leadership, you will notice that your own sense of yourself as a leader increases. You will notice that your speaking and actions as a leader are more efficient. Upon reflection, you will see how your followership is more secure as a result of your own self-assuredness. You will experience the Etiquette of Leadership bringing quality to your guidance.

The practices of *The Etiquette of Leadership* will change your way of operating as a leader. They will modify the ways you think about yourself. They will modify the way you think about what is important. In this sense, you will discover for yourself new ways to conduct yourself as a leader, and you will see that the Etiquette of Leadership is much more than just a code of conduct or a list of manners, or a method of conducting oneself as a leader.

Imagine yourself coming into a situation, ready to lead. You are quickly evaluating what is going on; the dynamics, the personalities, the tasks. From our research and conversations with hundreds of practicing and aspiring leaders we have deduced that in that nanosecond when you pause to take the breath before you speak or you contract the muscles of your body ready to take the first physical step of leadership, four elements are coming together.

The first is that you are bringing to that moment all your understanding of the context: your knowledge of the situation; your experience that is relevant; the story you have created for yourself and possibly others about why this situation is important and why it requires your leadership.

The second is that you are bringing all your previous understanding of what is needed for leadership: your models, thoughts, frameworks, ideas on what works and what doesn't in your guidance.

The third is that you are getting deeply aligned with your intention for this situation: what you want; what is required right now and into the future; what you are committed to achieving; what you think the outcome could be; what is possible for your leadership.

The fourth is that you bring the depth of your desire to make your intention be translated into your concern for the situation and the people involved.

These elements are developed in more detail later.

The way these four elements come together in that nanosecond before you speak or act is determined by the unique way you have chosen the Etiquette of your Leadership.

Chapter 1

LEADERSHIP ETIQUETTE

"Nothing is less important than which fork you use. Etiquette is the science of living. It embraces everything. It is ethics. It is honor." Emily Post, the doyen of good manners, said this about etiquette in American society in the 20th century.

Leadership is a science; it is about developing a hypothesis, setting an aim, collating the resources and methodically taking action. Once the leadership action is complete, we analyze our results, draw conclusions, learn and gain an understanding of what the next steps are.

Leadership is also an art. It requires an awareness to understand the context (the canvas). It requires a trust in our ability to draw on all of our experience (how we hold the brush) and conviction that the action we are about to take, provided it is done with care, is right for that moment (the brush strokes that go towards making the picture).

The Etiquette of Leadership is the science and art of moving oneself or others to action. The Etiquette of Leadership is the art and science of leading well. It is the act of accomplishing a change in state in another or in a situation that could not have occurred but for our good leadership.

From our research and experience, we have seen that several underlying tenets and principles inform the active practice of The Etiquette of Leadership. They are outlined below. We encourage you to begin to practice thinking about them by using the four elements we raised above as you consider each one. We also invite you to consider them separately and then begin to draw them together. In approaching them this way, you will start to build your unique Etiquette of Leadership.

A way that we have found that works well in doing this work is to read each section and have a notepad with you to jot down thoughts and ideas. This way you begin to develop knowledge for further development and reflection as you go.

▸ TENET 1: You matter

When we say *you matter* we mean this in at least two senses.

The first is that The Etiquette of Leadership starts with you. You are tremendously important to the successful outcomes of great leadership in the circumstances of life that you find yourself. You must lead yourself. Before you can lead others, you must first lead yourself. What does this mean?

It means that to lead yourself you must engage in the discipline and practice, what Post calls the *science*, of sorting yourself out. This must be done before you seek to lead others. The consequences of not doing so are dire.

The ranks of so-called leaders who have not engaged in this work, who have assumed that their position makes them a leader, are legion. Disasters follow in their wake: in their personal lives, in their relations with others and in their organizational outcomes.

Having engaged in this work, the benefits of finding yourself as a leader are enormous. If you do this work, you will discover and validate for yourself that the image you have of yourself as a leader is the primary determinant of how great you will be as a leader and how effective your leadership will be.

You must have an identity for yourself as a leader. You must know who you are. You must create yourself as a leader. Before others can see your leadership, you must know who you see yourself as and how you see your leadership being presented to others. This also begins to give you understanding for your followership.

Some ways to develop and refine your concept of your leadership self are presented below. If you are unsure of your Identity as a leader and feel that you don't have anything yet like a concept of yourself as a leader, please go to Appendix 1 where you will find the outline of a process for identifying and confirming your leadership identity.

The second sense of the phrase *you matter* is: it's not about you. This may seem strange given what we just said—that the Etiquette of Leadership starts with you. You matter. Leadership starts *with* you, but at the same time, it is not *about* you.

There is a paradox to be wrestled with here: You have to do the leadership work on yourself before you seek to lead others. And the focus of attention should not be about you. The Etiquette of Leadership concerns you, but it is not *about* you.

If you need work on yourself, because you are insecure or you have a condition that impacts on the effectiveness of your leadership, you can still exercise effective leadership and even be masterful in the Etiquette of Leadership. However, we say that to be maximally effective, you must first deal with that situation before seeking to influence, guide, lead, mentor and coach others.

The world is full of people who can't lead themselves and yet they seek to influence others, as if their own issues and problems, their own insecurities, doubts, foibles, bad habits, poor personal standards, past misdeeds and the like won't intrude into the next situation. Your issues and problems need to be addressed and are a part of your leadership journey to resolve.

These problems concern you and they need to be dealt with or at least begin to be addressed, so that they do not get in the way of your exercise of the Etiquette of Leadership. Before you start on the journey of effective leadership, you need to count the cost of ensuring that they won't intrude into your leadership in such a way that the situation becomes about you. In the moment that what you are doing or saying as a leader becomes about you, you lose the impact of the Etiquette of Leadership in that situation. Furthermore, your effective leadership itself is likely not to achieve all or any of what it possibly could.

When we talk of addressing and dealing with your issues and problems, we think in terms of being aware of them and having an intention of addressing or dealing with them. You are on a journey, so even as the leader, you're not expected to be perfect. The thing that matters is the effects, impacts, results, and outcomes of your leadership on others. Even if you are self-leading, i.e. seeking to provide leadership to yourself in a situation, the focus should always be on others; on what will move others to a new place that they could not have attained without the leadership you provide. If you reflect for a moment you will be able to recall people you have worked with, amazingly able people whose leadership always fell short just because of this one flaw—they let themselves get in the way of their leadership.

You will be able to recall pictures or stories in your experiences of people in leadership positions where their leadership fell short; didn't resonate, lacked impact. The reason is often that, in the saying and the doing of the leadership act, the focus was on themselves. They were over-thinking about what they were saying or doing, how they looked in the moment, how they sounded, whether their voice was strong enough. It is likely that they lacked the competence or capability to do this work. While they are incapable or still building their expertise, they are pre-occupied with the technique rather than the impact; they are thinking about their part in the leadership situation to the detriment of the impact their leadership acts could be having on others.

Your effective leadership, exercising the Etiquette of Leadership, will occur if you take on building the skills and then practicing them to the point that you feel—and you can witness for yourself in the results you achieve—that you have mastered them. At that point, your leadership will be like any great teacher who creates successful acts in partnership with another. The act of leadership will occur to you as one of grace, accomplishment, and ease.

To take an example, your leadership will be like watching a game of catch. Many people think that the skill lies in catching the ball. In reality, as much if not more of the outcome of a successful game of catch lies in the skill with which the ball is thrown, making it easy for the catcher to catch it.

This is what your leadership will be like when you exercise the Etiquette of Leadership. You will act with such practiced skill that your leadership will land with or be caught by the other easily and maybe effortlessly, making it possible for them to have success in catching your delivery, in receiving your leadership and being enabled to act.

The Etiquette of Leadership is the practice of moving situations forward without it being about you. This means that the focus should be on others and the situation should work for the other. If it works for you and not others, then it is not leadership. If it works for you at the expense of others, that is not leadership. In that sense, your attempt at leadership has occurred at a cost to another. You have made them pay for your guidance. You have deluded yourself into thinking that you have invested your leadership into a situation; in practice though, it has occurred at a cost to others.

Here is an example: you as a leader want to get a result from engaging another to do something. If you get the result but the other person is left disengaged that is not leadership, and it has not been done with anything like the Etiquette of Leadership.

The best leadership occurs where the follower feels safe; at least safe enough to follow the guidance of another, in the moment. The situation itself may not be safe; for example, a building is on fire, and the leader is seeking to lead others to physical safety. The others will follow the leader to the extent that they feel they are being lead to safety. For the leader exercising the Etiquette of Leadership, this is paramount; you will be effective if the focus of those you seek to influence is on them and not you, to the point where they feel safe in offering their follower-ship to you.

Here is another example: what will you do and how will you manage your sense of yourself when others react *wrongly* to the exercise of your Etiquette of Leadership? Is it because you have been ineffective, i.e. you take responsibility, or is it just some random reason? In either case, your task is to respond *rightly* (not in a moral sense but in the sense of effectiveness) so that you can help the other person settle. They may learn something for themselves about life, their own identity and the Etiquette of Leadership, or they may not.

Of course, if your guidance is effective, others will notice you, but that is not the main game. The main game is about others. In practicing the Etiquette of Leadership, you will notice that you are efficient in your leadership. In many ways that is all that matters. It does not matter that you are promoting the idea of the Etiquette of Leadership. Your effective leadership is not designed to allow you to increase in stature or status in your community. It is not intended to put you above or beyond others. Your active practice of the Etiquette of Leadership is recognized in what others accomplish through your guidance.

The Etiquette of Leadership is partly concerned with how you prepare yourself so that you can prepare others to be effective. There are other aspects to it as well that we cover later but this is the first place for you to pay a lot of attention as you prepare to learn the Etiquette of Leadership.

A situation won't change for the better unless leadership is exercised effectively. This requires you as a leader to be ready in yourself and able to ready others.

At this point, we encourage you to reflect.

What do you notice for yourself in the idea that you matter? What do you notice about the first sense of this tenet? Who are you as a leader? How do you describe yourself? What are your characteristics as a leader? What are you known for as a leader? What do you want to be known for as a leader in the future?

What then do you notice about the second sense of this tenet? If your leadership is going to be effective because it is not going to be about you, what do you have to deal with so that whatever that is won't get in the way of you effectively carrying out your unique Etiquette of Leadership? If it is something you need to address, how will you do so? Who will you work with to resolve it? If you are not going to address it, as a choice you make, how are you going to manage the issue so that it will not get in the way of your leadership? Who will you work with to handle the problem so that it doesn't get in the way?

Take time to reflect on this tenet. It is foundational to success. The reflection you do will pay huge dividends by giving you insights into your unique identity and how you are putting yourself together as a leader.

There is an excellent way to test whether you have achieved a balance in exercising the Etiquette of Leadership between the truism that you matter and that it is not all about you.

When you are involved in meeting others, say at a networking event, a meeting of a small or large group, a team production meeting or a social event like a dinner or a picnic with family and friends, notice whether you are thinking about yourself first and foremost or whether you can be aware of yourself but have the situation be about others and the situation that you all find yourselves in. If you can be conscious of yourself but not have that overbear you and the situation, you can effectively exercise the Etiquette of Leadership. In that moment, you can allow your awareness of the context of the situation be combined with the attention you are paying to others and their actions, words, needs and so on, and combine that with the elegance of how you are conducting yourself. At that point, the Etiquette of Leadership becomes a thing of beauty and effectiveness.

An effective way to build mastery in this is to practice. Begin today. Practice in small, insignificant situations where it doesn't matter if you realize that you are thinking only about yourself and not even giving a passing thought to others. Sometimes you will catch yourself thinking fixedly about yourself; in that moment, acknowledge it and choose to focus your attention where it belongs—on others. After a while, you will begin to take on thought processes and even body movements and voice tones that will be comfortable to you and will fade into the background, leaving you room to concentrate all your leadership on others.

▶ TENET 2: Your ethics determine the effectiveness of your etiquette as a leader

The second tenet that underlies this work you are about to engage in is that the Etiquette of Leadership is always and ever ethical. Ethics can be a complicated term and find its way into many complex considerations of life. Here, *ethics* has a simple meaning—to do no harm. If you exercise the Etiquette of Leadership ethically, you will be attuned to ensuring that no harm comes about to others, in so far as it depends on your guidance.

This is not to say that harm will never occur in a situation where you are the leader. Damage happens sometimes. Your role as a leader ethically exercising the Etiquette of Leadership is to give consideration and consciously exercise care for all the people involved in a situation, such that no harm occurs. Your role, your accountability, and responsibility is to think as well as you possibly can—in advance if possible—of what damage could happen and to think through what practical steps you can take to eliminate it.

When you lead well, ethically practicing the Etiquette of Leadership, people notice. They see the direction; their attention is piqued. They are aware that something has moved in the situation. They see you for what you have done in the moment. In the moment when leadership occurs people notice something new and extraordinary. When people see that what you are saying or doing as a leader is moving a situation forward and that no harm is occurring to anyone involved, they are enabled to follow you in ways that would not otherwise be possible.

The opportunity you have in becoming masterful in the Etiquette of your Leadership is to fill your life with many of these special moments. In that sense, The Etiquette of Leadership enables leaders to live life fully. It might contribute to the ideal state of consciousness described by Frederick Nietzsche where we might live a fully-lived life such that we overcome anxiety or anxiousness about our death.

The slight overlap between ordinary Etiquette and the Etiquette of Leadership occurs here. Followers respect others who practice etiquette, and they behave better when good manners are demonstrated. This is an essential part of leadership; you raising the bar, raising the tone, increasing performance and bringing workability without harm to others. It is always an option as to how to lead, but effective leadership situations are unlikely to occur when you do not display ordinary etiquette.

Let us illustrate this point with an example: *the use of humor and the use of strong language in leadership situations*.

If you practice common etiquette, you won't be seduced into believing that you can use inappropriate humor or language.

You will have noticed for yourself that if you do, the person you are seeking to lead will momentarily become frozen, stiff; maybe even recoil physically from you even to the slightest degree. Their attention becomes focused on the jarring nature of what has been said. It is as if they have become momentarily derailed. This is not usually likely to be an ethical practice. The reason is that, in the telling of the joke or the use of language, you have caused harm in the sense that they have lost their access to the larger effect of your leadership.

Of course, it may be that language and humor in one situation that is not ethical is perfectly okay in another, because it does not harm the responsiveness and *followability* of the person you seek to lead. If you tell a bawdy joke or you swear, and you conclude that it has done no harm, but you see an adverse impact on others, then it is not ethical—it has harmed them. And remember the Etiquette of Leadership is about others, not you.

There is a situation where you might seek to masterfully exercise the Etiquette of Leadership in an ethical way that is actually designed to momentarily derail the other. This can occur where you need to prepare the other person to shift their awareness or understanding. You want them to hear what you say, interpret it momentarily as being jarring or derailing for themselves, and while that is occurring, you prepare to move them carefully and ethically to another position in the conversation or action. The point remains, though; if it harms the other, your language and jokes are not ethical. You will not have exercised your Etiquette of Leadership effectively.

In the moment of leadership, at least one person—ideally you, if you are seeking to apply the Etiquette of Leadership—understands what to do in the moment, and you do it with four background factors that allow others to respond so that the relationship can be developed or the action can occur. These four factors were outlined in the introduction but are repeated here for ease of reference.

The four factors that come together in the moment of leadership are:

Awareness of the context, i.e. awareness of the background and the foreground of the situation and the size of the story that has been created to allow the situation to be understood and appreciated.

As an effective leader exercising the Etiquette of Leadership, you will have an appreciation of the wider situation. You will be able to describe that in terms that engage those you seek to lead. You will be able to put it in words or pictures that they can relate to and which will cause them to see the relationship between the wider picture and the situation that you are seeking to lead them through. Since most leadership acts occur to move a situation forward—to create action, to change the current state, to relieve the distress of the present situation—the context you create for your followers is likely to be significant enough that they will realize quickly that to remain stuck in the present will not be sufficient. They will begin to align with your picture of the context so that they are becoming ready to engage with you and move forward with you.

Understanding of your own frames and ways of being as a leader, i.e. your mental models, theories, teaching and training, experience in leadership to date, reflection and the like.

Some leaders, in simpler times, used to be able to lead just through their physical presence, prowess, good looks, muscles and such. If they made a case to move, others followed, sometimes out of fear but sometimes at least because of what they leader stood for and represented. In our modern life, models and theories perform somewhat of the same function; they serve to create a basis for followers to follow because they can see that the model or framework that the leader has is worthwhile and is more likely to lead to success. Models also serve a fundamental purpose for us as the leader; they give us anchor points and springboards for our thinking. They provide the basis for us to test the reality of the current situation. They can also help stimulate our thinking to new levels of effectiveness and sophistication.

Intention, i.e. both your intention about the situation in which you find yourself—e.g. *to create new energy in the team sufficient to get the bridge built one week earlier than originally planned*—and your thoughtful awareness of the expected effects of what you are about to say or do on the other.

There is an old saying: "If you don't know where you are going, any road you take will get you there." Having an intention that is real and has been assessed by you as a leader as worthwhile is absolutely necessary for successful leadership. Imagine a situation where a solution to a social problem like an outbreak of heat stress in the population during a heat wave is possible. Your intention could be to relieve the symptoms for those in a one-kilometer radius of your office and who can afford it. You will get a far different outcome if your intention is to relieve it for the whole population with a specific intent of ensuring that the most vulnerable are treated first, and that preventive steps are put in place at the same time as curative approaches.

Care for others. The aim of the Etiquette of Leadership is to prepare you so that you can care adequately for another. This requires you to identify and practice how to know and experience the other person as fully as possible.

Care has two deep meanings in the English language. It can mean looking after someone or something—*I care for you* or *I love you*. It can also mean in that same sentence something entirely different—*I care for you and your safety*. This connotes paying attention to the other, being aware of the other and expressing care as an act of intention; paying attention to another's welfare or a situation they are in.

The Etiquette of Leadership practices care as an amalgamation of both those meanings; *I care* is intended to express our awareness of the other person or the situation *and* our intention to do good, so far as we are able, in ways that contribute to the other or improves the situation.

Now, this might seem arrogant; us attempting to influence the life of another or the situation that has developed quite well enough on its own so far without any need for intervention on our part. The nature of effective leadership is that it chooses where, when, how and who to impact in a useful way and then acts.

So, *care* is much more than looking after another. It is more like *loving* the other, but that is such a meaning-loaded term that we hesitate to use it here.

The moment of leadership brings together your awareness of the context, understanding of your mental models, your intentions and your care. This is the culmination of the Etiquette of Leadership, where what happens is the result of who you are as a leader and how you set up what will happen next. It is in the careful execution of these four factors that mastery of the art of leadership comes about.

There is another aspect to the consideration of ethical leadership. We said above that, "If you exercise the Etiquette of Leadership ethically you will be attuned to ensuring that no harm comes about to others, *in so far as it depends on your guidance*."

To successfully execute the moment of leadership, bringing together these four elements, there needs to be a decision made in terms of taking responsibility.

Please do not fall into the seductive trap of thinking that you can ethically exercise the Etiquette of Leadership effectively by foisting the blame for harm on to others. So-called leaders who seek to blame shift when damage occurs are not leading—they are scapegoating. They are just following orders or advice of others, which starkly exposes that they are not leaders. They are admitting that the end justifies the harm and is thereby somehow excusable. They are seeking to maintain their lead at the expense of others.

Blame-shifting is an endemic practice in leadership. It is widely accepted and even endorsed, but it is unethical. If you cannot work out a way to exercise leadership without harming others and without having to shift the blame for harm to others, work out another way forward. There will always be one. It will perhaps require you to call on your deepest private reserves and insights, to cooperate closely with others to find a new way forward, to delay or accelerate action as required. But there will *always* be another way.

You may be thinking, "But there will always be situations where action has to be taken or statements made by me as a leader where harm will occur." You might even think of past situations or stories where leadership has had to happen, and something has happened that has caused damage. We allow the possibility that such cases can arise, but we challenge you to design your leadership from the perspective that so far as you possibly can, you will lead without harming others.

Deciding to exercise the Etiquette of Leadership is deciding to take responsibility. You have decided that you are taking on the responsibility of direction and all that it entails. It is only when you have chosen to take on that responsibility that you will be able to truly act ethically.

▶ TENET 3: Your principles; the knives and forks for the Etiquette of Leadership

The whole purpose of the Etiquette of Leadership is to help you create the best possible conditions for your leadership to be effective.

The principles that underlie the Etiquette of Leadership are the same as for etiquette—respect, considerateness, and truthfulness.

Leaders who excel are those who skillfully and sincerely apply understanding in their interactions with others.

The Etiquette of Leadership captures the wisdom of years of studying what makes for effective leadership. There are some common threads with the ordinary understanding of leadership, which will support you, as you understand and master them. There is also something totally unique about the Etiquette of Leadership; it is entirely unique for each active leader. The etiquette of your leadership shares many aspects of ordinary leadership in common with other effective leaders.

It will also be your unique expression of who you are as a leader and how you exercise the Etiquette of your Leadership efficiently. As you practice the Etiquette of Leadership and take on the attitudes that underpin it, you will increasingly be able to see their impact in the conventional practices that good leaders exhibit. You will also see it for your own leadership in the impacts which your particular approaches have on yourself and others.

Principle 1: Respectful leadership is what works.

Consider the impact of being respectful of yourself and others. Respect is demonstrating your admiration for someone's abilities, qualities, or achievements. Respectful leaders are also respectable, i.e. they establish the conditions that allow others to offer them their respect.

In their consideration of others, respectful leaders take on the mantle of putting themselves in the other person's shoes before they act. They consider the other. They place themselves in the shoes of the other. They respect the position, person, and place of the other, just because they can. Their approach reflects the words of an old song, "Before you criticize and choose, walk a mile in my shoes."

Being respectful is a precondition for the practice of common etiquette in life. It is part of being civil and living in a civil society. Leadership literature is replete with stories of apparently successful leaders who do outwardly unusual things at the expense of their followers, customers and other stakeholders—even society as a whole. There is an increasing trend towards this kind of disrespectful incivility in organizational life. It is not acceptable to act on the basis that because a person has regulatory power over another, they have the ability or even the right to act in ways that diminish others.

Respect of self and others has the most profound impact on who one is as a leader. Respectful leadership is what flows when we have a good grasp of the first tenet of the Etiquette of Leadership, *you matter*, and the theme we developed in that tenet—*it's not about you.* When we understand ourselves and our true relationship with those we seek to lead, being focused on them and not on us, we are in a place of great potential to crystallize the power of being respectful of others.

Here is a short story to illustrate the effect of the Etiquette of Leadership badly practiced.

"In my early days as a manager and as a person who leaders in the organization regarded as having career potential, I allowed myself to be

seduced by the idea that because I had been promoted to a senior role as a very young person, I was, therefore, a "someone."

There were obviously some good things I was doing to have others form a favorable opinion of me. But in my quieter moments of reflection (such as they were in a callow youth!), I recognized that there were things I was doing that seemed to be off-key with others.

In my arrogance and ignorance, one particular practice that came up for me was that of taking reams of papers from my in-tray to meetings. These were materials that usually had no relationship with the meeting subject at all. As the meeting progressed, I would plow through papers; noting, approving, forwarding or marking to be filed. I noticed that many of my meeting colleagues seemed puzzled by all this frenzied behavior, but I consoled myself with the idea that I could make productive use of my time by doing this stuff and still having the smarts to keep an ear on the conversations and discussions and make timely inputs.

I even used to do this during presentations by others where they would be standing at the front of the room, sometimes momentarily distracted by me shuffling papers and even distributing them to relevant others at the table.

Would you describe this as exercising the Etiquette of Leadership? To my shame, I later saw how disrespectful it was, to the chair of the meeting, to my colleagues and to presenters. The Etiquette of Leadership requires leaders to be fully attentive, respectful of the norms of the situation, showing respect to other meeting participants and presenters, fully participating in conversation and deliberation on the subjects for the meeting."

Respect sits alongside being considerate and includes being thoughtful, caring, even loving. It involves the notion of courtesy; the practice of polite behavior and courtliness. This is an area where the Etiquette of Leadership might factor in your experience. The etiquette of your leadership should be much more than being polite because politeness can so often be a sword. The word *polite* comes from the same roots as *politics*. Even if you are a political leader, you do not want to exercise political politeness if you are seeking to practice the Etiquette of Leadership. If you do, you will be acting, not living. You will be using the Etiquette of Leadership as a means to a political end. In so acting, you will deny the opportunity to be genuinely respectful in your leadership. In so acting, it will be about you and not about others.

Respectful leadership also allows no room for us as the leader to manufacture subordination. The leader who expects to use the Etiquette of Leadership as a tool to create subordinates will fail.

There is an excellent piece of Australian history that illustrates this point above. In the early years of the colonization of Australia by the British, Governor Lachlan Macquarie distinguished himself as a builder, a promoter of social good and economic advancement. His great flaw was that he required and demanded that every other person in the colony be subordinate to him. It eventually led to his undoing. All his good acts were diminished because of a sense by those he sought to influence through his governorship that they had to regard themselves as under his super-ordination.

This is an area where management can become contaminated by ineffective leaders who are not practicing the Etiquette of Leadership. Many managers act as if they are little gods. This is very often a result of the manager as a leader having a poor grasp of their own identity as a leader, misunderstanding the complicated relationship between their own sense of self and the respect that others deserve from them as leaders and managers.

Managers and leaders who adopt command and control approaches, who act politically, and who operate from their position inappropriately all serve to diminish the respect that their followers want to give them but do not because these actions promote fear, discomfort, unease and even sickness. When they act super-ordinately, they place themselves, their opinions, ideas, and intelligence above others in ways that diminish.

One of the great ways that we can build respect *from* others is to show respect *to* others. One of the best ways to do this is through the simple act of acknowledgment. By acknowledging someone's abilities, qualities, or achievements, we are simply showing that person that we see them. As described in the example above, a leader with followers he or she regards as subordinates drags behind them a tethered mass of disrespect—of their own creation. In the process of acknowledgment, a leader demonstrates their respect, connects with the individuals within their followership, allowing them to move to their highest point, inadvertently taking the leader and the rest of the followership with them.

Another way to build respect and to keep your own ethical edge sharp is to consider whether you should always speak respectfully about others. If you choose to take this on as a sound practice, you are likely to notice that it builds respect for you. When we hear a leader speaking disrespectfully about others, it often makes us uneasy. This is not only because of what is being said disrespectfully about the other person. It can also cause us to think fearfully about what that same leader might be saying disrespectfully to others about us. In the process of so doing, leaders practicing poor Etiquette of Leadership damage their own sense of respect. This process can become a vicious cycle.

In speaking respectfully of others and in seeking to acknowledge others there is some risk of appearing to be dishonest and untruthful. You will need to think this through for yourself. Our approach, as a piece of advice that you can consider and choose to follow or not as you desire, is that it is always more workable to speak respectfully about others. If we have to make *negative* assessments of others to third parties, we seek to confine statements to those that are relevant to solving an issue, not in gratuitously attacking the other person's character and reputation.

The Etiquette of Leadership acts as a guide for you as a leader in the ways you can demonstrate respect. It also serves another purpose; it facilitates the propulsion of the followership. By this, we mean that respectfulness creates alignment and unity so that those who follow you will want to be in action. Often the actions that your followers undertake will be propelled and accelerated because your followers will derive new energy.

At this point, we encourage you to reflect.

Before we conclude this piece, it is worthwhile focusing for a moment on how you apply the Etiquette of Leadership when someone you seek to lead breaches your understanding of what constitutes either common etiquette or the Etiquette of Leadership itself.

Say for example that you are leading a project to build a new structure. You have been working long hours, and there are many pressures building. In a project review meeting, one of the team members begins to speak angrily about the delays they allege have been caused by another team member.

Your capacity to respond as a leader exercising your unique Etiquette of Leadership gets to be tested right there. In many ways, this is the sort of situation that defines the Etiquette of Leadership and allows you to demonstrate your personal mastery of it.

What would you do in that situation? What would you say? Would you have confidence that the outcome of whatever happens next will lead to further productivity for the project team?

We leave this with you as a thought starter to bring home the immensely practical implications of this work for you in designing and practicing the Etiquette of Leadership for your own situation.

Principle 2: Considerate Leadership is what makes a difference.

Leaders exercising consideration in their Etiquette of Leadership intentionally create the conditions for others to do their best in response to the call or the situation requiring action.

We do this by being mindful of the state that the others are in and what we as the leader assess is going to be needed to bring effectiveness. That awareness or mindfulness can be gained through our senses and also our intuition. Here is an example.

Joyce is walking towards a group of people. She sees them milling around, she hears voices being raised. Some appear to be acting provocatively towards others. One person is lying on the ground. The movements of the group are staccato, abrupt. She senses there is anxiety, anger, upset. The situation looks potentially explosive; punches may start to be thrown any minute.

All these responses she has are considerations. She considers them. They may or may not be accurate since they are conclusions she has come to or possibilities she has entertained about the meaning of the situation. Whether she has accurately assessed the situation or not, she decides to act considerately.

She moves closer to the group. She listens. She hears one person speaking apparently aggressively to another. The rest of the team seem to be bystanders although some appear to be egging the aggressive person on. A couple of others are acting defensively, protectively towards the person experiencing the aggression.

Joyce moves closer, standing to the right of the aggressive person and potentially between what looks to be the two protagonists. She breathes in, aware of her own body position, calling on her inner resources to stay calm. She consciously lowers her speaking pitch and puts out her hand at waist level, palm down. She begins to speak and slowly moves further forward.

All these gestures and insights are part of her considerate leadership.

She has prepared herself for leadership by being considerate.

We can't know what the outcome of that situation will be, but we can be assured that her consideration of all the aspects leading up to her action has been made considerately. It is our contention that this makes a huge difference to the effectiveness of leadership in the moment. It is an example of the essence of the Etiquette of Leadership.

Considerate leadership also gives keen attention to the safety of the other, as well as self. This includes both physical and emotional safety. Leadership can be exercised in unsafe moments. However, they are much more likely to have beneficial outcomes if the safety of self and others is maximized in the situation at hand and in the thoughts the leader is having about what will happen next.

Considerate leadership allows the other to be free; free to act, think, respond, reply, build, connect or a thousand other responses. Freedom to react is a crucial part of considerate leadership. We allow others to process and respond to our direction by creating permission; permission for the other to be free. Our contention is that this freedom creates the opportunity for generative leadership. By this, we mean the transformational outcomes that occur when real leadership creates a useful and forward momentum in others that accomplishes that which would not otherwise have happened, but for that leadership.

Considerate leadership has almost, but not quite, no place for a desire to control. It may be a desire to control others or to control a situation. It connotes the idea that the leader is the only one who can determine what is morally right or wrong in a situation and that therefore the leader is justified in taking away the freedom to act. This is not part of the Etiquette of Leadership.

Followers will usually work and respond best to your leadership when you speak and act in such ways that your followers are released, enabled, feel respected and encouraged to move forward. The only exception we know of where control is sometimes the best form of considerate leadership is where the followers lack capability or competence to do what the situation requires. Then, the leader may need to direct and control.

The significant risk in always acting and speaking in a controlling or directing way is that it brings the focus of attention to the leader. If you choose to take that quality on as part of your Etiquette of Leadership, so be it. We find that the risks of ego, narcissism, and the like becoming dominant usually outweigh the possible benefits, but we encourage experience, accompanied with reflection and intention to learn from that experience. As we said above, sometimes this is necessary, but it is more likely to occur in situations such as where your followers lack competency, or there is a real emergency.

It is also likely that leaders who habitually seek to control others lack care. Sometimes it is masked in paternalistic thoughts and ideas. But it is usually tough to be a controlling leader and at the same time to be a caring leader, to exercise respect and esteem, and to speak and act in such ways that you do not make others fearful because of your attention to their frailties and shortcomings.

If you think about situations where you have operated in this way or have experienced leaders who have acted in this way towards you, you will notice that this behavior creates dependency. It forces the creation of adult/child relationships, which might be appropriate if the leaders were an adult and the follower was a child. It is an approach that is unlikely to be effective in the longer term between two adults or a leader and a group of adults.

A useful adjunct to this idea above occurs when we, as leaders exercising the Etiquette of Leadership, realize the power to be had as a leader when we speak and act so as not to make the other feel or consider themselves wrong, lacking, falling short or not being up to the mark. Situations may create these conditions—people never do. Or, at least the other needs to be assured that the situation has resulted in an unfavorable state but no matter how bad it is, the person is not themselves *wrong*. They might see for themselves that they need to change or make other decisions to affect the situation. But real leadership is most likely to occur when the focus is on the situation to be addressed, not on the innate quality of the other as a person.

Considerate leadership happens when we act so elegantly that the response of others is to be drawn to us, seeking to do what we propose or agree with what we say, or at least give it consideration. The Etiquette of Leadership does not hold room for creating an impression in what we say and do that the other must do something to win our favor or come up to our standard as access to having our acceptance. We do not hold to the idea that embarrassment, belittlement, isolating and the like are acceptable approaches in the Etiquette of Leadership. We hold to the idea that our behaviors are most likely to be focused on creating *we* rather than *I* and *you*.

Now you have read this far it may appear to you that the ideas of respect and consideration seem to overlap—they do. There are also some differences. Respect is essentially about valuing the other person for who they are. Consideration is about appreciating their situation. When we exercise the Etiquette of Leadership considerately, we are considering the circumstances of the situation that we find ourselves in. We are applying our awareness. We are continuing to take in and process the signals. We recall the important pieces of data about ourselves, others and the situation that will allow us to act effectively.

Then when we speak or act, we are doing so with consideration.

At this stage, it is important to note that when considering a person or group's situation, care needs to be exercised to know the fine line of passing judgment. A considerate leader will put themselves in somebody else's shoes, to gain an understanding of their situation. The Etiquette of Leadership takes the leader a step further.

When gaining understanding for someone's situation, it is important not to make judgement about that situation—things are where they are. This is the element that creates freedom within your consideration for others. As a leader practicing the Etiquette of Leadership, the next step you take is to determine how your actions can create a safe experience that allows that person to grow.

In addition to being considerate about the circumstances that have lead up to the moment of leadership and the present moment itself, we also are considerate of the future. What could be the outcomes of our words and actions in exercising leadership? What will the impact be for others and ourselves?

Much of the commentary about the practice of leadership focuses on the outcomes in terms that do not include the impact of our words and actions on the state of others. The focus is often on getting the job done, with little or no thought as to the overall impact on others. When we act considerately with the Etiquette of Leadership we are deliberate and give conscious consideration to where the others are going to be left emotionally, physically and spiritually by our words and actions of leadership.

We may not be able to predict or control the impact on others in advance. All the planning and thought we can possibly do is unlikely to always and forever determine the outcome. But the process of giving consideration can improve the likelihood of effective outcomes.

Our impact can be so much greater if it is considered in advance. It can also be greater in the moment if we are consciously paying attention as we are moving our lips or exercising our muscles in leading. Paying attention, being aware and considering others can allow us to make small or large alterations to our delivery in the moment to increase our effectiveness.

We have a mission with regard to exercising the Etiquette of Leadership with consideration. We can know that we are leading considerately when we see that we are operating and others are responding, and the overall effect is that leadership is being exercised with no harm. This is a crucial element in acting with consideration.

To circle back to earlier material, leading with a conscious consideration of seeking to do no harm involves respect and ethical dealings. It also reflects your desire to act wisely. It is not always possible to prevent damage, but it should always be your aim to ensure no harm is done, so far as you humanly can.

There are great warrior stories of impassioned leadership speeches such as those that occur in wartime. You can imagine the scene where the leader is about to sound the charge to battle, and he rallies the troops, ready to go over the top of the trenches and off to an almost certain death. These situations do occur. But except in the most arduous times of war, they do not happen in reality, even in the armed forces, except in the most exceptional circumstances. Today, modern military leaders spend enormous amounts of time and effort planning to ensure that no harm is done in action. This quality of consideration gives troops in war a heightened sense of respect and trust; knowing that their leaders have considered every possible factor to ensure no harm comes to them.

If this is the case in theaters of war where real physical harm and even death can occur, how much more relevant is it in modern workplaces? Good leaders do not trifle with their followers' safety. They seek always to ensure that no harm is done as a result of actions that have to occur.

When we are planning a leadership act, especially regarding a significant matter that will impact on our followers' lives, we owe it to them to plan to do no harm. If our leadership actions have repercussions for others' emotional and physical safety, we are obligated and motivated to prepare thoroughly to minimize the adverse results.

So far, much of this section has been focused on considering others. We can do ourselves a great service too as leaders if we give consideration to ourselves—the impact of what we say and do on ourselves.

Much of the present dysfunction that occurs in organizations today is directly attributable to the failure of leaders to be considerate to themselves. This is not a call for giving managers more money or larger offices, more so that good leaders know the impact of their leadership on their own emotions. They act considerately of themselves by engaging in activities such as enlarging their emotional intelligence, practicing awareness training, debriefing with a competent coach or another professional support person, even rewarding themselves for a period of high performance with some extra sleep rather than merely continuing at a frenetic pace.

At this point, we encourage you to reflect.

Here is a great test of whether you are exercising this tenet of consideration in your practice of the Etiquette of Leadership; notice how you respond to others who display some kind of weakness. It might be a physical weakness, it might be a weakness of intellectual grasp, or it might be something as simple as the weakness of another in not knowing what to do in a particular situation. If you act graciously, generously, understandingly, considerately you should notice that you create a much better likelihood of moving a situation forward than if you do not. This is a real moment of leadership; what you do in the face of another's weakness.

If you are exercising consideration as part of your Etiquette of Leadership the other person keeps breathing regularly and deeply into their stomach; if they continue to feel safe and that you have been considerate of them they will tend to breathe low.

What do you notice with yourself when you are considerate and when you are not?

Principle 3: Truthful leadership is what endures

In the writings of etiquette teachers, you will see their reference to the importance of honesty in etiquette. The good host is said to be able to speak honestly about a situation and also always uphold the other tenets of etiquette.

In the Etiquette of Leadership, we have redefined and sharpened this idea. Some bad leaders would take the concept of honesty and use it as an excuse for poor speaking or conduct. Being *honest* can easily be misused as an excuse for being brutal or hurtful of the other.

Our conception of this principle is enlarged to add truthfulness to honesty. Someone speaking honestly speaks earnestly, deliberately, keeping to the facts and the like. Someone speaking truthfully speaks what is true. There are many philosophical distinctions regarding the notion of truth. We intend it to mean something quite specific here. By *truth,* we mean being sure, as designed, as planned, right, ringing true. Some would include the distinction of *integrity* as another way of describing truth as we are outlining it here. We say that truth in the Etiquette of Leadership encompasses all these elements.

We have purposefully listed truth thirdly in the list of principles because the truth is powerful and it needs to be supported by respect and consideration to have a real and positive impact. Without the other two principles in the mix, damage and devastation can be left in the wake of truth. When, as a leader, you stand in the truth of the situation there is power; it is the simplicity of truth that gives it its power. No one can whittle it away; it doesn't need your justification, it can just *be*. Even though there is a simplicity to the truth, the important thing is how it is delivered, and this is where respect and consideration come into play.

The old saying *truth hurts* doesn't have to be right. An influential leader, with experience of the Etiquette of Leadership, will know how to deliver truth and demonstrate its power graciously that will lead to the followership emulating the practice.

We also add another element to our conception of truth in the Etiquette of Leadership. It is acting in such a way that the other will respond to our leadership with trust and fidelity. The greatest moments of leadership occur when we lead, and others respond by putting their trust and confidence in us. This is an enormous privilege granted in the moment of truly effective direction, and it comes with how the power of truth is being handled. The trust of those who follow our leadership is code for them feeling secure in what we have said or done, or propose to do.

In that moment of trust, another great thing happens—others give us their fidelity. Fidelity is an old word connoting loyalty and faithfulness. Dogs are said to be paradigms of loyalty to their owners. We don't want to create situations where followers act obediently and ingratiatingly towards us. We want them to respond with a great and genuine sense that what we are leading them about can best be responded to with their honest and enduring support. When that happens, they will be confident in the outcome we are leading them towards. In that circumstance, they are willing to give us their trust.

Good leaders practicing the Etiquette of Leadership speak and act truthfully. We say what is so. We go where we intend to go. We move as planned.

Our words and actions bring truth. In speaking and acting truthfully, we reinforce the tenets of respect and consideration. They all combine to bring progress and advancement to a situation.

At this point, we encourage you to reflect.

When practicing the Etiquette of Leadership, what does it feel like for you to speak and act truthfully?

Can you recall a time when you have acted against the truth, in an attempt to achieve the desired outcome, appease someone or simply disregard the potential impact of taking this action? What happened? What were the levels of respect and consideration received from your followership? If you still received the same degree of respect and consideration, how did that make you feel?

There are times when many of us feel or think little about those "white lies" or sentiments of "what people don't know won't hurt them," but practicing the Etiquette of Leadership is not only about that one moment. It is also about a journey of mastery; it is not only about your journey, but it also includes those of your followership, those you interact with and those that come after you.

Respect, consideration, and truth are fundamental principles that will help keep the pathway of your journey clear.

Chapter 2

THE ETIQUETTE OF LEADERSHIP IN PRACTICE

So, the moment arrives when you have decided to lead in the particular situation you find yourself in. In that moment, you have made a *choice to decide* to be a leader. You could have chosen lots of other ways of being in that moment. You could have been content to be a bystander, a passive person, maliciously compliant, a second-in-command or deputy leader. You could have been a resister, a revolutionary, an analyzer, an assessor, a judge, an adviser, a commentator, a functional resource or whatever. But you have chosen to be a leader, and in that moment, you have also made a decision—to lead and not to be a non-leader.

In that moment, you create yourself to be something and someone unique—the leader for the moment. It will never occur again just like that. In that moment, you have "murdered the alternatives," which is what *decision* means in Latin. In that moment, all your preparation for leadership comes to the fore. If it has been preparation appropriate to the needs of the situation, you are likely to lead well and exercise effective leadership. You have decided that you matter, but it is not about you. You have chosen to lead ethically, you have decided to act on your principles, and importantly, you have elected to take responsibility. You will have identified your identity as a leader. You will have thought about and selected for yourself your moral bearings, what you want to work at as you exercise respect and consideration, what difference you are committed to make and what truth you will bring to light.

The Etiquette of Leadership is firstly about that preparation for the moment of leadership that will give you the result you are seeking.

The Etiquette of Leadership is much more than common etiquette for business, family or community situations. It assumes you know about how to behave in meetings, how to sit, how to engage in conversation effectively around the dinner table. It presumes you know how to be polite, what to say in moments of difficulty, how to address the Queen, how to hold your knife and whether it is okay to tuck your napkin into your shirt.

In addition to how you prepare for the moment of leadership, The Etiquette of Leadership is also about your presence. By this, we mean not just being *physically* there but also how you show up; what you say and do in the moment, and how you move things forward so that your leadership makes a positive difference in a situation.

So, the Etiquette of Leadership starts with who you create, construct or design yourself to be as a leader. It focuses on the moment of leadership. It then develops into the outcomes of the moment. In all these instances, the Etiquette of Leadership can guide you how to exercise, in a practical way, who you are, how you want to be and give you confidence in what you need to do next.

The Etiquette of Leadership is a way of living and working as an effective leader. (see Chapter 7: The Etiquette of Designing Yourself as a Leader).

It also encompasses a series of practices which are intended to increase the effectiveness of your leadership. No matter what training, capacity building or competency increasing you have done already, the Etiquette of Leadership aims to complement wherever you are now and allow you to take your leadership to new levels of effectiveness, elegance, and attractiveness.

When people see this leadership in effect, they will also see that it is your practice of the Etiquette of Leadership that has created these outcomes. The Etiquette of Leadership allows you to be wherever you are now as a leader and to increase your awareness and reflection so that you can design the next level of effectiveness and then practice it in real life leadership situations.

As you read on you may see for yourself practices and ways of being as a leader that you have been engaged in which are different from what you have been doing or being in the past. You are encouraged to see these potentially new practices as insights for workability; consider trying them out as new ways of accessing effectiveness. At no stage are we seeking to have you consider past practices as *wrong*. They may have worked, or they may have not worked for you in the past. The Etiquette of Leadership is not about making yourself or others wrong; it is about learning from experiences, creating opportunities and demonstrating a form of leadership that is tailored, unique and practiced by you in a manner that is respectful, considerate and truthful.

At this point, we encourage you to reflect.

In the following chapters, we present material as to how the Etiquette of Leadership can be acted upon in the entirely different situations of work, in social settings and at home. As you will see there are common themes but also some particular nuances of how The Etiquette of Leadership works.

Take this time now to think of a leadership scenario which you have experienced for each of these areas of your life.

Having these experiences at the forefront of your mind will help you think about how you have practiced the Etiquette of Leadership, how you could have practiced the Etiquette of Leadership in those situations and what way you may implement the Etiquette of Leadership in each of these areas when the next leadership moment arises.

Chapter 3

LEADERSHIP AT WORK

The Etiquette of Leadership might seem at first glance to be about where most leadership articles, blogs, and books are focused at present—work. Work is a big part of where the Etiquette of Leadership can be practiced. Work is also the place where effective leadership is most greatly needed. The paradox seems to be that the more that is written about leadership at work, the less efficient it is becoming. The Etiquette of Leadership seeks to break this pattern of ineffectiveness.

As well as in work situations the Etiquette of Leadership can also be brought into your social life, your family life, and your community life. Imagine your good leadership, exercised effectively through the practice for the Etiquette of Leadership, making a difference in all these areas.

A useful way to think a bit more deeply about this and to combine it in a slightly different way is to consider the Etiquette of Leadership existing like a three-dimensional, triangular pyramid, with three points at the base and an apex.

The first point on the base is *activities*. This includes all the tasks you do, procedures you follow, the values you operate to, the strategies you fulfill, the dreams you work towards, the promotion you are desiring, the rewards you enjoy from your job, etc.

The second point on the base is *leadership*; the skills and practices you perform that enable you to move an action forward in a way that would not have happened but for your guidance.

The third point on the base is *care*; the interest, compassion, concern, desire, etc. you have for another and the situation which is presenting itself in the moment. It is the essence of the respectfulness and consideration you are bringing into the situation.

The fourth point, the apex of the pyramid is your sense of yourself—who you see yourself to be. This also offers you the opportunity to give thought and find understanding for your connection to your work; e.g. your connection to a work setting could be ambition, curiosity, the challenge and experience, or simply, and perhaps more commonly, financial.

When all these four points are being brought into action effectively, your unique Etiquette of Leadership is present in and for you. By *present,* we mean things like "in existence," "having been created and constructed" and "worked on and honed to its current point."

The action of leadership at work can include so many different environments, situations, and relationships. This next section seeks to outline some of these variables to allow you to reflect on how you might apply the Etiquette of Leadership in any one or all of these circumstances.

Let's jump straight to the bane of everyone's workplace—the meeting.

Joyce calls a meeting and immediately the usual complaints, groans and sighs arise throughout the whisperings of the office.

"What a waste of time."

"Another session of all talk, no action."

"Here we go again; can't wait to hear what today's rant is about."

Joyce hears the tail ends of conversations and picks up on the negative vibe. With an understanding of the Etiquette of Leadership, she sets about preparing for her meeting. This is an example of the science side of the Etiquette of Leadership.

Joyce begins by going back to the start, *Tenet 1: You matter*. She knows and has made the active decision that she wants to be and is a leader; so now she thinks, "How can this meeting help me create or reinforce my leadership identity?" Joyce remembers these statements: "You matter," and "Leadership starts with you, but it's not *about* you." This reflection causes her to remember and jot down a few prompts on the agenda that will remind her of her essential characteristics as a leader. She writes:

"Need team to understand and be accountable to achieve the proposal."

"Listen for the unsaid."

"I will always seek to move the conversation forward," and,

"Keep my ego in check!"

Knowing who she wants to be as a leader, Joyce then sets herself the task; what can she do in this meeting that will result in an outcome where everyone can benefit?

Now Joyce starts to think about what specific actions she could take within this meeting, keeping in mind *Tenet 2: Your ethics determine the effectiveness of your etiquette as a leader*. Joyce understands that this tenet is of particular importance when it comes to meetings, and knows that it is important to remember that if she exercises the Etiquette of Leadership ethically, she will be attuned to ensuring that no harm comes about to others, in so far as it depends on her leadership.

With the meeting about to start, Joyce has decided to exercise her leadership; she knows who she is and wants to be as a leader and that being a leader is not about her. She has decided to be an ethical leader; so now comes the detail. Joyce thinks, "How do I *be* this leader?".

This is where Joyce thinks about and implements *Tenet 3: Your principles, the knives and forks for the Etiquette of Leadership.* Joyce imagines herself about to sit at the meeting table and about to engage in the meeting rituals in the same way she would if she was about to sit down for a fine dining experience that same night. She can see the options open to her in the meeting much as she can envision the knives and forks for dinner that evening. She is about to pick up the meeting equivalent of one of the sets of knives and forks that are laid out in front of her at the table, but which to choose?

Joyce recalls the simple rule of thumb for the etiquette of formal dining; start from the outside and work your way in with each course. She knows that so too with the principles of the Etiquette of Leadership, a simple rule of thumb can be called upon. Each principle is meant to be used and can be utilized in the order she has thought about them already.

Joyce continues preparing for the meeting and then when she sits at the table, she knows to be respectful, give consideration and be considerate, and be truthful as a specific way to reinforce her sincerity.

Joyce realizes that her leadership will reveal her principles. It exposes who she is. Also, having knowledge of who she is and what she wants will not only allow her to lead with confidence but will also inspire her followership to accompany her on the journey.

The outcome of the meeting is that Joyce lifts the energy of the room, engages with participants, facilitates active participation and creates tangible actions with precise results and expectations, well within the timeframe of the meeting. Those who have been given the responsibility for individual tasks take ownership; those who haven't know how to support and everyone is clear on their roles, responsibilities, and contributions.

It is easy to talk about preparing for a meeting but what do you focus on? The content? The outcome? Do you just show up and wing it? Through the Etiquette of Leadership, you take a holistic approach and take care of all of these aspects, but the focus is not on you; it's on your followership and the attention and intention you have for them.

Here's another example practiced by one of the authors. He has distilled his Etiquette of Leadership for meetings into a simple yet powerful statement that he often recalls before, during and after his leadership at meetings and other work activities.

---

*"Put people first, have fun, and the work
will come in off to the side."*

— *Ben Baldwin*

Ben's unique Etiquette of Leadership works for him.

We give these two examples to show that there is no prescribed way to develop your unique Etiquette of Leadership. We suggest you try a few approaches and experiment until you start to find a suite of strategies that work well individually and in combination for you.

The approach taken by Joyce for her meeting is an approach that can be taken for other work-related activities; seminars, board presentations, stakeholder meetings, etc.

This is where the *art* of the Etiquette of Leadership comes in. It's like choosing your medium—paper, canvas or wall—and then knowing and making the necessary adjustments for the context.

Another context to consider executing the Etiquette of Leadership is the times when you need to manage up, a concept which in relatively recent times has become an acceptable and practical concept to engage. However, to effectively manage up or even across, particularly in a hierarchical organization, you will need to have a thorough understanding of the tenets of the Etiquette of Leadership and be prepared and confident in the demonstration of the fundamental principles, acting with respect, consideration, and truthfulness.

It is a common misconception made about leadership that you have to be in a hierarchically appropriate position to be a leader. The Etiquette of Leadership can be practiced by anyone who has decided to be a leader; it is not dependent on your position in a company, how many people report to you or how long you have been around.

A good example is when Joyce decides to lead without authority.

Following Joyce's meeting, one of the decisions agreed by her team is to suggest changes to the executives of the organization that would allow the successful delivery of the outcomes Joyce and her team have been given the responsibility to achieve.

The preparation Joyce has undertaken, leading up to the team meeting has already equipped her for the follow-up meeting with her boss, one of the organization's executives. In this situation, Joyce will now need to give some further consideration to the principles that will help her execute the Etiquette of Leadership, while up managing her boss.

Principle 1: Respectful leadership is what works. Joyce understands that the organization relies on its hierarchical nature, perhaps a little too much, so a clear demonstration of respect will be required.

Joyce decides she will demonstrate her respect for her boss, the hierarchy and the organization within their meeting and will act with transparency. She will be consistent with her behavior in terms of how she approaches, communicates and interacts with her boss on a daily basis and will operate with no agenda, but will have specific outcomes from what she would like to achieve in the meeting.

As a leader demonstrating the Etiquette of Leadership, Joyce decides that she will connect with her boss in a manner such that she is inviting them to become a part of her followership, allowing them to move to their highest point, inadvertently taking the leader and the rest of the followership with them.

Joyce is lifted by the thought of inviting her boss to be a part of her followership, knowing that she can demonstrate a form of leadership that transcends hierarchy. Her intention is to bring all involved along on a successful journey, and all those people have wins that create the desired outcome for the benefit of each individual and the organization as a whole. But how will she achieve this?

Principle 2: Considerate leadership is what makes a difference. Joyce recalls that leaders exercising consideration in their Etiquette of Leadership intentionally create the conditions for others to do their best in response to the call or the situation requiring action.

Joyce gives thought about what the situation for her boss might be leading up to their meeting; e.g. what's on their plate? What pressures might they be under or what do they think about Joyce and her team? How might he receive the information she is about to hand over and what are the possible outcomes? Joyce knows that by giving these things considerations, she is making judgments and assumptions; while we say that it is important not to make judgments, it is more that it is important not to *stay* in judgment. To move yourself to the point of view where you can freely think, "things are where they are." With this in mind, Joyce's considerations will create a sense of freedom for whatever is going on for her boss, the current situation, and the organization.

As a leader practicing the Etiquette of Leadership, Joyce's next step is to determine how her actions leading up to and within the meeting can create a safe experience that would allow her boss to expand. Joyce has decided that through her leadership within the meeting she will demonstrate a style of considerate leadership that has given keen attention to the safety of the other person as well as herself and team. Joyce knows that by acting in this manner, she will give her boss the freedom to act, think, respond and make decisions that have a value and impact far more prosperous than any individual could create themselves.

Principle 3: Truthful leadership is what endures. Joyce is absolute in her resolve to be the best leader she can be, demonstrating the Etiquette of Leadership wherever possible, but she believes that for her leadership to be successful, the outcomes of each of her leadership moments need to be felt, believed and trusted.

Joyce elects to speak honestly at the meeting with her boss, committing herself to be earnest, deliberate and keep to the facts. Further to that, Joyce is confident within herself to speak about—and wants to be recognized for speaking—what is known to be true. By enacting the Etiquette of Leadership, Joyce has decided to take responsibility for each leadership moment she commits to and to act with integrity.

In these moments, Joyce is establishing trust, and when this is obtained, Joyce knows that it requires ongoing maintenance and care from which others will give their fidelity to her leadership.

Joyce conducts the meeting with her boss. At first, she is a little nervous, but before too long she has drawn on her understanding of the situation. She knows what is required from her own style of leadership, she reminds herself of her intentions and the purpose of the meeting, and finally, she is clear about her concern of the situation and the people involved, including her boss.

It would be great to hear that all went smoothly; the meeting was short, succinct and successful—however, that's not how it went arther the meeting went longer but more productively than either had anticipated.

Joyce's boss listened to her and had his reaction, but because of her preparation, she was able to respond in a confident, understanding and leaderful manner that allowed her to work with her boss to come through his reaction. Thanks to Joyce's leadership in that moment, together Joyce and her boss were able to develop appropriate actions for Joyce and her team to move forward. They were able to propose some measures that the boss could take back to his executive peers that would potentially lead to organizational changes for the benefit of Joyce's team, Joyce, her boss and the organization.

At this point, we encourage you to reflect

Can you think of occasions where you have been proud of your leadership and a situation where you have not been proud of your leadership? What was the difference with who you were, what you were thinking or how you acted on those two different occasions?

With what you have read thus far, how do the three tenets of the Etiquette of Leadership relate to each incident? What would you do differently?

Chapter 4

THE ETIQUETTE OF LEADERSHIP AT HOME

Several years ago, writers and commentators started talking about the "balance of work and life," as if work and life were somehow distinct.

Nothing could be more ridiculous. Of course, they are different situations, but there is one common factor—you. The Etiquette of Leadership that you exercise at home is the same that applies at work and in every other situation just with your partner, children or extended family, rather than colleagues.

Using the Etiquette of Leadership at home allows you to expand the experience of family; be present during times with your children and accept, acknowledge and reciprocate the love with your partner.

An essential connection that binds us at home is love. The Etiquette of Leadership, through the demonstration of each tenet and principle, will create new ways for you to express your love and experience love from your family.

From birth, we are surrounded by at least one person who sees us for who we are; it begins with either or both parents observing us grow and seeing and influencing our personality and our being as we get older. At some point, this mantle is handed over to a partner of our choosing. For the most part, we have chosen this partner, and they have chosen us because we have *seen* each other. And then as we get older, our children see us for who we are again. We say *again* because during our children's years of innocence they see who we are; they know when we are present and when we are being ourselves. They know when we make mistakes, and they know when we have made corrections, but we often don't think about our children being there for us during this time—we are there for them. We will also come across people in our lives that see us for who we are, e.g. teachers, friends, colleagues, and so you can also extend this concept to them if you are lucky enough to have these people in your lives.

I would like to share an experience of leadership as a father.

My son is nine years of age as I sit here and write this book. When he was three months old I decided to make some significant life changes so that I could be the person I wanted to be and demonstrate to him the benefits of being true to yourself, the possibilities of what our lives hold and the ability to make corrections should we find ourselves on an undesirable path.

During this time, I had found myself so deep in trying to achieve these things and always looking to what was next, that I wasn't being present for my son, my family and myself. I started to notice that during those times I wasn't present, my son would "act up," trying to get my attention. This would lead to me becoming frustrated, which carried over into other relationships within my family. But one day, someone spoke told me about being present, being in the moment and experiencing all that was to be experienced in that time.

So, I decided to start being present with my son. When he wanted my attention, I would stop what I was doing and be with him. Initially, I had to knock back thoughts such as, "I'll play in five minutes," "How long will this take?" or "I don't want to do that activity." So, we would play, we would make eye contact, we would talk, we would ask questions, and sometimes we would just play in silence; all the while my mind, focus, and attention were on him and this time. I soon noticed that he would have had enough time playing with me after a while—often shorter than I was ready for—and he was content in doing his own thing. He started to listen more, demand less of my time and stopped acting up, while I wanted to play more and actively looked for things that we could play with together. I also found myself creating closer connections with my partner; I was more present in everyday conversations with people, and I became more productive in my work. By practicing being present with my son, I started to be more present with other people and experiences as well.

This was my first experience with *Tenet 1: You matter*, and understanding that, while I set out to do something for myself and demonstrate leadership at home at the same time, it wasn't all about me.

I have always tried to act ethically, but have never thought about ethics within the home. So, when I think about *Tenet 2: Your ethics determine the effectiveness of your etiquette as a leader* within the context of home, I reflect on times when simple actions, such as being present were vital to being an ethical leader at home. And being present is only one aspect of leadership. When we are leading at home, we are leading at times and in ways that we are not necessarily conscious of, and our followership is those people who see us. By practicing the Etiquette of Leadership at home, keeping in mind our simple meaning for ethical behavior—*to do no harm*—allows us to demonstrate what we would like our home followership to be, create an environment for them to define and practice their own leadership and give them the opportunities to correct.

Our home setting allows us to an opportunity to be more vulnerable than in any other setting. Our connection to this setting is love and, to be sure that we look after this love, we need to be respectful, considerate and truthful. Being a leader at home affords you an opportunity to explore, demonstrate and refine *Tenet 3: Your principles, the knives and forks for the Etiquette of Leadership.* This is the Etiquette of Leadership in action; home provides you the opportunity to not only demonstrate leadership but also creates an opportunity for you to learn more about your guidance and have your family learn and experience leadership for themselves.

At this point, we encourage you to reflect

If we are now aware and accept that we have people in our lives, wherever we are in our lives, that see us, what do they see? What can we learn from them that would help us develop ourselves as leaders? What can they contribute to our practice of the Etiquette of Leadership?

By taking time and thinking about the tenets and principles of the Etiquette of Leadership in a home setting, we have the opportunity to find key answers that will help with our leadership mastery.

Chapter 5

THE ETIQUETTE OF LEADERSHIP IN SOCIAL SETTINGS

Leadership in social settings is an interesting aspect of life that is not given as much thought as leadership in other aspects of life, such as work and home, as previously discussed.

The Etiquette of Leadership is a practice that can be used in every facet of your life. In this section, you could consider social settings as events, e.g. business drinks, conferences, seminars, parties, ceremonies, competitions, networking and community events

So, what differs in a social environment, compared to that of a work environment or at home? What needs to change with the execution of the Etiquette of Leadership?

Very little!

The approach that is taken for you to continue your demonstration of the Etiquette of Leadership is largely the same. Perhaps one of the important differences is your connection to the social setting.

Your connection to a work environment could be ambition, curiosity, the challenge, and experience or a myriad of other reasons, but more often than not the primary *connection* to work is financial. So, when you are enacting the Etiquette of Leadership in a work setting there is often a level or risk, obligation and/or appropriateness that will play a role in when, why and how you implement your leadership.

On a similar note, your connection to home is most likely love. Here your own definition of love and what love looks like will play a role in when, why and how you implement your leadership.

On the other hand, social settings have an entirely different connection to you. Social settings are often something that you have decided to engage in freely and purely for yourself. These are the extracurricular activities to work, to home and your day-to-day living activities. You have chosen to be involved in a given social setting for any number of reasons, too many to mention on this occasion.

Your connection and attachment are personal to you, and your decision to implement the Etiquette of Leadership into this aspect of your life demonstrates your true desire to master your leadership.

You have come this far through the book and have by now grasped a firm understanding of the concepts we are delivering, and we think that this is a perfect place to ask the most important question of all. In this section, it is not so much about how to go about the practicalities of executing the Etiquette of Leadership, it is taking you back to a critical decision point. To engage your leadership or not engage your leadership.

There are many more freedoms in a social setting than at work or home and what often comes with freedom is the difficulty in decision making. For example, when we ask people if there were no considerations—money, location, training, etc.—what would your ideal occupation be? Many people have trouble answering this question. Within a social setting, we get a step closer to a situation that is not bound by consid-eration, remembering this is a situation that you have actively chosen to get involved with that doesn't have the same financial concerns as work nor has it the same implications of love, like home.

When you are given the opportunity to step into a leadership situation and engage the Etiquette of Leadership in a social setting, what do you choose to do? Decide to lead or decide to follow?

Thanks to Kenny Rogers, there is a fundamental question to ask yourself in the lead up to each leadership moment:

"Do I hold, do I fold, do I walk away or do I run?"

The following is an example of a thought process of deciding to lead in a social setting.

As a person who has chosen to master my leadership through the demonstration of the Etiquette of Leadership, striving to continually better myself and meet challenges head on, who is solutions-focused and looks for an opportunity, I have found it difficult to answer this question. In the past, and sometimes even now if I'm not quick enough to catch it, my mind goes straight into an analysis for an appropriate justification for the decision.

Am I bailing from this challenge?

If I just go for a little longer, I might achieve my win!

I have done so much, it would all be wasted if I didn't keep soldiering on!

What am I missing here? Surely, I just haven't found the right solution yet!

And the questions go on and on.

It seems the thinking I go through is to keep me in the current circumstance—my own fight against change.

Practicing the Etiquette of Leadership within a social setting allows me to play with my leadership, test my leadership style and reflect on how well it is performing and being received.

Fortunately, I have the support of a fantastic wife, the backing of a good friend and mentor and an understanding that I do have the capacity for good decision-making and capability to adapt to most outcomes. I also know that by following the concepts provided by the Etiquette of Leadership, whatever I choose to do will be respectful, considerate and truthful.

With this valuable pool of resources, I have the opportunity to explore and reflect on the given circumstance, better understand the situation and think about what I want my future to hold.

By dipping into this pool, I find that the line of thinking I previously described is not in present time. It is often thinking about the circumstance from when I first entered it; it doesn't take into account the actions I have taken, the outcomes that have transpired and how both the circumstance and I aren't in the same position relative to each other as we once were.

For me, it's another demonstration of the power of being present and the hint of me resisting change is the key clue that I am not in present time.

I realize that even during my involvement in a particular circumstance when I feel a decision point arise, I need to be in present time. I need to look at the situation like I am deciding to engage with it for the first time; this changes the set of questions I ask to help make the decision. Questions such as:

"Do I want to get involved?"

"What is the intention of my involvement?"

"What can I offer to this challenge?"

"What can this challenge offer me?"

"What do I see are possible solutions/opportunities?"

"What do I want as an outcome?"

So far and for the most part, this approach has helped a lot for a number of decisions I have made, where I can be objective within social settings, having more freedom to explore, experience and educate myself on what leadership is and how best I can action my own leadership style.

And it doesn't actually matter what the decision is. What I have found is that there is a level of leadership required on my behalf to execute my decision, and by implementing the Etiquette of Leadership practice I have been able to enact my decisions for myself, while ethically looking after others with respect, consideration, and truth.

To practice the Etiquette of Leadership within a social setting allows you to experience leadership in an entirely different way. It provides you an opportunity to explore your leadership style, trial different ways of being a leader and demonstrate to others the possibilities of leadership.

At this point, we encourage you to reflect.

What is the key driver/s for you in your social settings? Do these social settings require you to lead or follow? Do you exercise the Etiquette of Leadership within these settings?

A social setting provides you an opportunity to explore and test the Etiquette of Leadership for yourself in a safe environment. Investigating your leadership in a different arena of your life will allow you to find answers that will contribute to leadership mastery.

Chapter 6

THE ETIQUETTE OF BEING A REFLECTIVE LEADER

Plato attributed Socrates as saying that an unexamined life is not worth living.

To practice the Etiquette of Leadership effectively you must first be prepared to be self-aware and accept the responsibility that that awareness brings. The only way to be self-aware is to reflect. Reflect on who you are as a leader. Reflect on your leadership in your life as you look into the future. Reflect on what you did today as a leader and what you can take from the situations you encountered.

We have alluded to this throughout the book, through the inclusion of reflection points at the end of each chapter.

Now, let's use reflection to understand its power and its importance.

Recall the first tenet of the Etiquette of Leadership, *you matter*. We discussed that there were two senses of this tenet; the first is that the Etiquette of Leadership starts with you. The second is that leadership is not about you. The difficulty with this doctrine lies in finding the balance between concentrating on yourself, working the world out for your own journey and being available to others to help them with their mission. The way to find this balance is through reflection.

When we talk of reflection in terms of the Etiquette of Leadership, we think in a way that is holistic; your reflection involves you and those you lead and interact with in the past, present and future. Just by reflecting on your own actions and thoughts to a given situation won't help you master the Etiquette of Leadership. You need to take a big picture approach, reflect further on how your actions and thoughts have been received by others, and how the actions and thoughts of others have impacted you. Then we ask you to go further again and reflect on how all these interactions influence your future self and others. Through this reflection process a series of questions can be called upon to help you find your balance. What is the outcome you see and is this the outcome what you want? Is it a result that aligns with who you are and what your leadership is about? And have you allowed yourself to matter, while at the same time understanding that it is not all about you?

So, while reflection is about you, it's about you wanting to learn from the past so that you can be aware now of being present in the future. It is also about you in relation to others.

Reflection allows you to be your own referee. This is where you matter; not how others judge you, but how you judge yourself. Giving consideration to *Tenet 2: Your ethics determine the effectiveness of your etiquette as a leader* during your reflections will allow you to take the extra steps that will give rise to a deeper understanding of yourself, your actions and your thoughts, honing your mastery of the Etiquette of Leadership.

As we mentioned in Chapter 1, when you lead well, ethically practicing the Etiquette of Leadership, people notice. The moment of leadership brings together your awareness of the context, understanding of your mental models, your intentions and your care. This is the culmination of the Etiquette of Leadership, where what happens is the result of who you are as a leader and how you set up what will happen next. It is in the careful execution of these four factors that mastery of the art of leadership comes about.

Reflection is a process that creates an opportunity for you to review your performance of the execution of your guidance. Like the video referee in sport, you can make an appraisal of your actions and thoughts with clarity, from different angles, make reference to your own rule book and then decide to make a call. The decision could be to play on or to take a penalty, learning from an action or thought that in hindsight doesn't meet your own ethical standards or accept the win.

But you need to be aware if you are being ethical and you need to be aware when people notice.

This is where *Tenet 3: Your principles, the knives and forks for the Etiquette of Leadership* can guide you with your reflection. Leaders who excel are those who skillfully and sincerely apply understanding in their interactions with others. But to achieve understanding, you need to be able to draw on your ability to reflect. We have highlighted that three principles underlie the Etiquette of Leadership—respect, considerateness, and truthfulness.

When taking the time to reflect, these policies need to be in place. You need to be able to have respect for the actions, thoughts, context, and outcomes that occurred at the time you are reflecting on. It is important to recognize that, in this moment of reflection, you and those you were interacting with were operating according to what they were aware of that time. You need to be considerate, be easy on yourself and those you were interacting with; take this opportunity during reflection to give consideration to new elements of the moment that have come to your awareness. Hindsight now gives you time to give additional consideration to how interactions have played out. By revisiting the outcome, you can learn how your actions and thoughts and those of others contributed to it, and what you may want to do differently in terms of how you may execute your leadership in the next moment it is called upon. Finally, you need to be truthful. Reflection is a process that is personal to you; it is your choice whether or not you share your observation with others, but it is important to be truthful to yourself. This is where the mastery of the Etiquette of Leadership sets its seeds.

This is what draws together a followership: if people can feel that a leader is willing to be truthful about themselves to themselves, then they can believe that this same leader will be truthful to them.

The power of reflection can be demonstrated by this following example.

Joyce had started a new job, a job that she had been striving for. A position within a large multi-national organization, working for an employer that looked through her CV and saw who Joyce was, saw her skills and capacity and saw how she would thrive within the team and work environment. Joyce was six weeks into her new job and a new job offer was presented to her, and Joyce gave this proposal serious consideration.

During her consideration, Joyce suddenly became aware how ridiculous it seemed to be thinking of a different job when she had only just started her *dream* job—what was going on? Joyce decided to take some time to reflect on this. Was she not happy? What wasn't her dream job giving her, that she expected to receive? And what kind of behavior is she displaying when she is obviously not showing commitment to her dream job?

Joyce's reflection revealed to her that she wasn't being herself in the dream job; at some point, she had decided to let others lead, and she would be passive in this new environment. She saw that, while a project was going pear-shaped, others would know better; she's only new, so what would she know? She let her herself become the lackey, after spending so many years being proactive, crafting her leadership, being leaderful and being true to herself.

Joyce realized that for some reason she had lost her balance with *Tenet 1*, she let others matter more than herself; she saw that she believed that in a large corporation she didn't matter. Joyce could see that she had started to ignore her own ethics. Joyce was aware of why the project she was on was failing but by being passive was allowing the potential of harm to others. By not acting on her awareness the project could fail, resulting in a myriad of negative consequences for individuals, teams and both organizations involved in the project. Joyce became aware through her reflection that she was not standing by her own principles. She was not being respectful to herself; by playing a role that was submissive to her own being, Joyce was not being considerate to her team by not actively contributing, drawing on her experience, trusting her capabilities and being leaderful. By acting in this manner, other members of the team were having to pull her weight as well as their own to progress a failing project. And Joyce was not being truthful; by not being herself she was letting herself down, potentially creating the *wrong* reputation about herself and not giving her dream job the chance that she deserved.

With this newly gained awareness, through reflection, Joyce decided to respectfully decline the new job offer, to be her proactive self and actively contribute to the project she was on.

Now I would like to say that all was rosy; however, while overall the learnings for Joyce were positive, she had still created a bit of a mess that she had to clean up. There was some work to be done to turn the project around, her team took a little while to trust her, and the final quality of the project wasn't up to her usual high standard. But through further reflection, Joyce was able to come up with a method of how she would do things differently next time, and during debrief meetings with members of the team, she shared her reflections and thoughts which enabled people to get their own insights and understanding for what occurred during the project. Many liked the method that Joyce had developed and are looking at how they might create something similar for themselves, to be able to work within a project their way.

Reflection is a way to refuel yourself on your leadership journey. It allows you to pause for a moment, look back from where you have come, appreciate where you are and remind yourself on where you are planning to go. During times of reflection, it allows you to examine what you are taking with you on your journey and decide if you need it or not. It lets you choose the path you want to take, and it allows you to re-inspire yourself, giving you the opportunity to recall your motivations for the journey you have decided to undertake.

Reflection can be a powerful learning tool. It allows you to embrace your journey and build awareness. Awareness brings responsibility. How you handle that responsibility will allow you to choose how you carry forward your unique "Etiquette of Leadership."

At this point, we encourage you to reflect

Do you take the time to pause and reflect? How do you go about reflecting? Is it through a diary or through conversation or through some sort of meditation? Do you get refueled by your reflections?

Take the opportunity right now to reflect on your leadership journey, this time keep in mind the three tenets of the Etiquette of Leadership—refuel yourself.

Chapter 7

THE ETIQUETTE OF DESIGNING YOURSELF AS A LEADER

The Etiquette of Leadership encompasses three domains: Who we are as human beings, what we are doing as leaders and the results that flow.

Who we are as people has a profound impact on who we are as leaders. Who we are as leaders influences how we exercise the etiquette of our own unique leadership.

There are billions of ways we can be human; that is why each of us is unique, although there may be patterns that describe us. Our unique humanity influences the ways we exercise our leadership.

When you are a leader, you are continually transforming yourself through your awareness of who you are in the world and the impact you are having on situations and others. Our contention is that who you are being will determine what you do as a leader and how you exercise the Etiquette of Leadership.

This premise underlies Tenet 1 of the Etiquette of Leadership, *you matter*. At this point, we would like to take a further dive into this concept and help you untangle the idea that within leadership you matter, but it is not about you.

You are tremendously important to the successful outcomes of great leadership in the circumstances of life that you find yourself. You must lead yourself. To do this, you need to understand who you are as a leader.

With the knowledge of who you are as a leader, you will be more comfortable with the second element of Tenet 1—leadership is not about *you*.

You have to do the leadership work on yourself before you seek to lead others. And the focus of attention should not be about you. The Etiquette of Leadership concerns you, but it is not *about* you.

Consider someone who knows all the good manners of leadership. Even if they are not aware of who they are as an underlying state or way of being, their hidden character will still be evident.

For example, I may know how to speak in a leaderful way at a public meeting so that I convince others to support my position on a topic. But if my underlying way of being is different from what I am saying, it will come out in the way people react and respond.

Here's a deeper example. I go to the meeting. I get a chance to speak. I say things powerfully, persuasively and logically. I appeal to the emotions and interests of the listeners. They applaud. I sit.

Have I exercised the Etiquette of Leadership? If my underlying way of being is manipulative, insecure, insincere or lacking personal commitment and the like I will have exercised my Etiquette of Leadership in an entirely different way than if I was being committed to being inspirational, to genuinely listen to the underlying sentiment of the meeting and to allow my grounding as an individual to be openly shared with others listening.

The complication that arises in much of the debates and literature about leadership at this point is that many argue that it doesn't really matter what approaches you use as a leader, as long as you get the result you intended. They say that the end justifies the means. This is said to be especially so if the stakes are high. This is the point where you have the opportunity for yourself to determine your own stance.

At one level, the Etiquette of Leadership says that each of our own approaches is unique and valuable and should be regarded as such by us as individuals and by those with whom we are in contact.

At another level, we are seeking to indicate that some practices of the Etiquette of Leadership are likely to not only fit better for most of us, but they are also likely to produce better outcomes. You may choose to have a way of being that others describe as *manipulative*. In the face of that description, you might opt to maintain the ways that manipulativeness is expressed. You may modify it in some respects, or the very description of an approach as manipulative might cause you to reflect and develop another method. All three responses are valid. The thing to consider is not only whether you will get the result you intend, but also whether you will get it in a way that is consistent with who you want to be in the world.

We do not prescribe a particular approach as being *the right way*. What we have found is that there are groups of understandings and approaches about leadership that, when practiced well, produce outcomes that promote the exercise of leadership and achieve better results than others. We cannot say that there is one prescription. We cannot say that any approach you adopt is right or wrong. The only question we can pose is, "Does it work for you?"

The answer for you depends on your chosen way of being in the moment when you draw in a breath to speak or take the first step forward into action.

What is your way of being as a person who exercises the Etiquette of Leadership?

Our contention is that you do not have to be any particular way of being; it is your choice.

You will find that ways of being have a tendency to cluster themselves around two domains; the one described below is what we would call the domain of being required for the efficient exercise of the Etiquette of Leadership. There is also another domain which we simply call *fear*. This domain is not described further here, but if you are interested, you could construct for yourself the ways of being that characterizes this domain and decide for yourself the implications of those ways of being for your own leadership. Our further contention is that leaders whose way of being is drawn from the domain of fear are unlikely or unable to exercise the Etiquette of Leadership effectively.

There are literally thousands of ways of being. Here is a list of some modes of being, below.

Respectful	Mindful	Involved	Forgiving
Considerate	Courageous	Consultative	Unresentful
Thoughtful	Energetic	Acknowledging	Preserving, building, maintaining, sustaining
Caring	Peaceful	Inspired, inspirational	Sociable
Loving	Present	Truthful	Ethical
Gracious	Transcendent	Simple	Generous
Mannerly	Transformational	Inquisitive	Fully (self) expressed
Kind	Revealing	Accepting	Self-empowered

Helpful	Disclosing	Connected	Ataraxic (being serenely calm)
Supportive	Opening up	Informative, informed	Curious
Resourceful	Creating	Spirited	Intrigued, intriguing
Mobilizing	Exploring	Spiritual	Reflective
Communicative	Unconstrained	Prayerful	Active
Relational	At rest	Future-oriented	Composed
Authentic	Trustful	Pain free	Committed
Vocal	Verifying	Sincere	
Contemplative	Leaderful	Faithful	
Aware of self and others	Intentional	Self-believing	
Fully alive	Available	Self-confident	

Our suggestion is that you go through the list in a relaxed way, savoring each term and reflecting on its meaning to you. Note the ways of being that you respond mostly to. The number is not important. Deepen and develop your own understanding of the meaning of the ones you choose.

We then recommend that you describe for each a couple of instances where you can recall having been that way.

Then identify a number of cases in the future where you could take on that way of being.

For example, I might define *being considerate* as a way of being that I want to continue with and to develop further. I recall that I was being considerate when I took on the coaching of a friend of a friend who was really struggling in their life at the time. I acted out of considerateness in offering to coach them through a particular issue they were facing.

I might choose to develop my way of being considerate further. I can foresee a conversation I could have today with the lady who helps my wife with heavy cleaning at our home. I could take on having a conversation with her about her daughter who has contracted a rare illness and ask her what assistance I can provide of a practical or supportive nature.

Here are the beginnings of a possible list of ways of being. As we said above, it is just a start. Add your own. Choose those that interest you and develop them further as suggested.

There is a whole group of ways of being that begin with the prefix *en* or *em*. These come from Latin, through French to English, in the main.

They often denote the idea of putting something into or onto a person or thing. They also signify adding to or bringing into a new condition or state. These are wonderful ways of thinking about who you are as a leader; creating whole new conditions or states, bringing whole new ways of being for yourself and others to the fore.

Engaged	Energizing	Ennobling	Envisioning
Enlisting	Enlivened	Entrusting	Enlarging
Enrolled	Enhancing	Encouraging	Endearing
Enabled	Enterprising	Ensuring	Entertaining
Enjoying	Endowing	Enriching	Enthusiastic
Empowered	Emergent	Emotional	Emboldening
Employed	Emitting	Emotive	Empathic

Another way you can access your ways of being is by identifying the ways of being that may not be part of the way you want to be.

Here are some:

Annoyed	Untrustworthy	Fanciful	Humble
Angry	Pompous	Pollyannaish	Reticent
Fearful	Deluded	Self-effacing	Stuck
Treacherous	Craving	Shy	Immobilized
Verifying	Painful to self and others	Reluctant	Ignorant
Unaware	Uninformed	Role dependent	Positional
Cynical	Maliciously compliant	Non-conforming	Embarrassing

You should notice that these ways of being are not necessarily right or wrong. Some of them have moral tags to them. The more efficient way of considering your values is to work through them and identify those you can see will work for you, and those that will contribute to your effectiveness in exercising the Etiquette of Leadership.

These various ways of being, in turn, give us our values. What deep values do you distil from your ways of being?

For example, your values might include being committed, having integrity, being in communication, being authentic and being in service of others. This then might transfer into the values of living fully for yourself and others, being fully attentive to others and enjoying the complexity and richness of a varied life.

What are your ways of being, values, and platform for the Etiquette of Your Leadership? Once you have explicitly identified them, you can use these values as the platform to design what you do.

There is a lot of commentary about values in leadership. It's hard to comprehend how a leader could lead without having some values at least at an unconscious level. The value of values-driven leadership lies in making our values as leaders explicit for ourselves and then capable of being modeled and shared with those we seek to lead.

Values sharing is a practice you might care to consider for your own Etiquette of Leadership. In the process of developing shared values in teams, for instance, alignment can be increased, accountability and support can be built.

One of the reflections we have about values in leadership is that very often the values that we develop for ourselves are those who are missing in our present practice of leadership. As an example, in considering a situation, you might identify ethical dealing as a significant value. You might identify that because it is actually something that is missing from the situation at present. As a leader, you take action to increase the value's presence in the situation by dealing ethically yourself, calling out unethical practices, addressing systems that lack ethical processes and practices, etc. In the conduct of these actions, the value of ethical dealing becomes *valuable* to you as access to your active practice of the Etiquette of Leadership. Once the situation has been dealt with, the value of ethical dealing might diminish because in the next situation you face it is not an issue for you to address as the leader.

As the leader, you may want to make sure that individual values are strongly in evidence in everything you and your followers do. In this sense, they become foundational or core values that are part of your identity as a leader and as a team.

In your leadership, you will also notice that the values you have identified as being important for yourself are not always and forever practiced. The *value of values* is that when they are not practiced or are not in evidence, they do not need to act as a weapon to be used to beat yourself up for not *living the values*. Like many of the other aspects of the Etiquette of Leadership, values not practiced serve to point us as leaders back to where we need to go to get back on track. Sometimes this will involve acknowledging, seeking forgiveness, making retribution, apologizing, providing redress or making right the damage done.

Once this work is done, the original values can then be reflected on and either confirmed or modified for future leadership situations.

Having worked out your way of being as a leader, you are then in a position to exercise, conduct, carry out, do, perform, action, act upon and bring into effect.

We provide more material in the next chapters about this aspect of the Etiquette of Leadership; the situations we find ourselves in and how to conduct ourselves. In preparing yourself for this work, we encourage you to do so with high-quality thinking in advance. It is not always possible to do this, and it is not always the approach that some of us as leaders prefer.

Sometimes a situation arises where careful preparation cannot be done. In an emergency or when a previously unthought or even an unthinkable event occurs, the full depth and quality of the Etiquette of Leadership emerge. This is where the leader is tested in the moment. When you have a well-developed sense of the Etiquette of Leadership for yourself, you will be able to accomplish actions in the emergency situation that you would not have been able to do had you not done this work.

We said above that thinking in advance is not always an approach that all leaders feel comfortable with. We who are introverts tend to think before we act, so it comes more naturally often to think about the situations we believe will arise and prepare ourselves in terms of what we will say and do. In such preparation, we know that things may not actually turn out as thought. However, the preparation is likely to put us in a place of being able to adapt, adjust, modify and alter as required by the situation at the time, certainly more than we could have done if we had not thought and reflected in advance.

For those of us who are more extroverted, who talk and act as we go in order to clarify our thinking, this preparation can be more of a chore. However, we encourage introverts and extroverts to do this work as much as you feel comfortable doing. This is because it will increase the impact and effectiveness of what you go on to do in the situation.

Chapter 8

THE ETIQUETTE OF LEADERSHIP IN WHAT YOU DO AND SAY AS A LEADER

Based on who you design yourself to be as a leader, you are now in a position to appreciate the Etiquette of Leadership from the standpoint of who you are. You should now have a deeper understanding of the first tenet, *you matter*, and a clearer understanding of when we add *but it's not all about you*.

From this point, having designed and understood who you are as a leader, you are in a better position to appreciate yourself and your leadership potential.

From this platform, you can now transition into what you will do and say as a leader exercising the Etiquette of Leadership, leading to a further exploration into *Tenet 2: Your ethics determine the effectiveness of your etiquette as a leader.*

As previously described in earlier chapters of this book, ethics can be a complicated term and find its way into many complex considerations of life. Here, *ethics* has a simple meaning—to do no harm. If you exercise the Etiquette of Leadership ethically, you will be attuned to ensuring that no harm comes about to others, in so far as it depends on your guidance.

Your role as a leader ethically exercising the Etiquette of Leadership is to give consideration and consciously exercise care for all the people involved in a situation such that no harm occurs. As with the section above on possible ways of being as a leader, here is a table of possible ways of acting as a leader ethically.

Focusing on "we" not "I"	Speaking in different ways e.g. creatively, motivationally	Consulting others	Serving
Creating the sense of "we are all in this together"	Following other leaders	Problem solving	Opening up- removing constraints or obstructions. Making a path
Listening	Leading the way forward	Inspiring others through acts of service	Reflecting
Responding	Counseling necessary caution	Offering e.g. healing, teaching, resources, care, acceptance	Accomplish-ing - obtaining, securing, getting, achieving
Acting, as in activity, not acting out	Considering before proposing or acting	Uncovering the future	Serving

Opening up - removing constraints and obstructions	Resourcing	Sacrificing	Overcoming fears and doubts through a way of being
Calculating	Evaluating risk and opportunity	Searching for what is possible	Sticking with others, being with them throughout whatever happens
Marshalling resources	Keeping spirits high	Not making others wrong	Encouraging
Displaying courage	Responding to changes in context	Staying true to ideals and values	Showing the way
Making space, creating a place	Enabling self and others e.g. building resilience	Exercising discretion	Planning

Having chosen how you will translate your being as a leader into moral actions you could take as a leader, you may be confronted by the realization that you don't yet have the skills to actually *do* the actions. The Etiquette of Leadership embraces a whole raft of practices. Coaching, training, advice giving, mentoring, thought partnering, consulting, etc. can all be useful tools for acquiring the skills you need to be able to competently act.

If you need to gain inputs from others to build your capacity to act, we offer a word of advice; choose providers who you are confident will support you in exercising the Etiquette of Leadership: someone who aligns with or demonstrates your desired ethics, values and principles.

A good way to select a coach or other personal adviser is to assess how well they practice the Etiquette of Leadership in their work and life before you engage them.

When you know who you are as a leader and you are translating this into your actions, you will progressively see that you are able to powerfully engage others at the level of their being.

Imagine the increased effectiveness that flows to a situation when it is transformed from someone standing at the front of a space giving an order, to a conversation like this. "We are faced with this situation. I am committed to being A, B and C. I am asking for your support. It will require you to be A, C, and G. If you are able to be that it will require us to do 1, 2, 3. Can I count on you?" If they respond "Yes," then you say, "Let's go." You speak to their way of being from your way of being. In the act of speaking and acting you ignite for them the possibility of confirming or transforming their way of being.

You can exercise the Etiquette of Leadership in your actions even if you are not the formal leader of a situation. In any given day, there are situations where you will be a formal leader, an informal leader, and a follower. You can exercise the Etiquette of Leadership in your ethical actions in all these situations.

Chapter 9

THE RESULTS OF YOUR ETIQUETTE OF LEADERSHIP

Who you design yourself to be and what you take on to do will give you precise results.

If you create yourself to be a person who effectively exercises the Etiquette of Leadership, you are likely to accomplish otherwise unachievable outcomes. By understanding and demonstrating *Tenet 3: Your principles, the knives and forks for the Etiquette of Leadership*, in concert with Tenets 1 and 2, you will contribute to improvement, transformation, benefit, enrichment and sustainability. You will overcome.

The results that flow from what you do are determined by who you are, your ethics and the demonstration of respect, consideration, and truth. Keeping in mind that respectful leadership is what works, considerate leadership is what makes a difference, and truthful leadership is what endures.

Here is a list of possible outcomes.

Clarity	Direction	Alignment	Followership
Fellowship	Progress	Achievement	Acceptance
Endorsement	Commitment	Prosperity	Peace
Fulfillment of plans and expectations	Completion	Relatedness	Accomplishment
Contribution	Outcomes	Fulfilment	Outputs

In exercising the Etiquette of Leadership, always keep in mind that while there will always be outcomes or *haves* from who you are being and what you are doing, you will sub-optimize the haves if you focus on them for their own self and for your own self.

Here is an example that relates to the outcome of contribution, in the list above. If you focus on the rewards like recognition, celebration, sense of accomplishment, promotion, publicity and so on, for their own sake the results will always be less than you could have attained if you focused first on who you are, then on what you are doing and lastly on what the outcomes are.

The reason for this is that those we seek to lead can always see where we are coming from. Your followers have a built-in antenna to pick up on a self-focused approach to rewards. They will always contribute less than they could have contributed. They will not feel safe in your leadership. They will feel controlled and manipulated.

The Etiquette of Leadership explicitly excludes the possibility that the end justifies the means. The outcome you desire will be much more efficient if it is accomplished with good Leadership Etiquette.

Chapter 10

ASSESSING YOUR MASTERY OF THE ETIQUETTE OF LEADERSHIP

If you have taken the trouble so far to clarify your identity as a leader, where you are going to exercise your leadership and how you will express care in your guidance, you might now like to ask yourself: Where am I in exercising mastery in my Etiquette of Leadership?

The Etiquette of Leadership is not like a competency test: it is not a case of you being assessed as *competent* or *not yet competent*. Mastering the Etiquette of Leadership can be a lifelong journey. It is a continuum. One way to determine the level of your Etiquette of Leadership is to consider it in the following terms.

▸ Level 0

⊙ I'm interested in the Etiquette of Leadership.

⊙ I see the benefits of the Etiquette of Leadership in my own life.

⊙ I have practiced leadership occasionally.

- I wonder about how to move forward.

- I have a leadership title but realize that it doesn't make me a leader.

▶ Level 1

- I have built a statement of my leadership identity.

- I have a role where I can exercise leadership of others.

- I have a clear sense of when it is appropriate for me to lead and when to be a follower.

▶ Level 2

- I have a plan to develop my leadership.

- I regularly work specifically on my leadership capabilities.

- I have been recognized by others for the direction I have brought to specific situations.

▶ Level 3

- I am fully engaged and have substantially completed what I have planned, to build my Etiquette of Leadership.

- I notice that when I offer leadership, others follow. I am consciously practicing followership.

▶ Level 4

- I have worked on my leadership journey for enough time to know that I am a leader.

⊙ I am put in positions because of my recognized abilities as a leader.

⊙ I am a mentor to others who seek me out for leadership support.

▸ Level 5

⊙ I have the ability to transform followers into leaders.

⊙ My leadership is credited as the reason why significant difficulties in a range of situations have been resolved.

⊙ I am working out my own Etiquette of Leadership in advance of the situation, watching myself practice it in the actual situation or moment, observing the impacts of it on the others and reflecting and refueling afterwards.

⊙ My family recognize me as their leader and are grateful for it.

If you have made it this far, congratulations! The culmination of all your thinking and consideration of this significant volume of ideas is to give you a practical experience of the Etiquette of Leadership. If you have thought sufficiently well to achieve an understanding of yourself that you are happy with you will be now able to see what the ideas being the Etiquette of Leadership amount to. They can be summarized as follows.

"As Etiquette is the science of life, and Leadership is the art of wisdom and awareness in action, the Etiquette of Leadership is the art and science of ethically leading a life of wise action."

If you can see that you are ethically leading a life of thoughtful action, you can consider yourself as having mastery of the Etiquette of Leadership. If you are not yet there but are committed to staying on the journey, you will continue to see benefits flow to the quality of your life and the impact you have on your followers and the world.

Chapter 11

WHAT REMAINS AFTER YOUR LEADERSHIP

Much of the commentary about leadership is focused on preparing for and conducting leadership acts. Little or nothing is devoted to planning for what will remain after you have spoken or served as a leader.

Consider a situation where you are planning to exercise the Etiquette of Leadership in the near future. What will be left behind after you have spoken or acted? How will your leadership have impacted the underlying situation that required leadership? How will those who have heard you or acted on your leadership be left?

It is probably never knowable in advance, in precise detail, how others will respond to your guidance.

They may be unmoved, passive, unengaged or not committed to any extent to respond.

They may be actually turned against your leadership, resistant, antagonistic, outraged or maliciously compliant.

Or they may be moved to action by your leadership, responding, creative, exercising their own initiative to achieve a now shared objective, active, seeking to engage others and preparing themselves for whatever is required.

If you choose to apply the Etiquette of Leadership, you might experience any one of these outcomes. To the extent that it depends on you, the types of outcomes will tend to be more favorable, but there is no necessary guarantee. This is because followers will always respond in ways that work best for them in the situation.

While you cannot necessarily know how others will respond to your leadership, it is incumbent upon you to plan how others, your followers, will be left.

Much of their response will be determined by the effectiveness of your Etiquette of Leadership in what you say and do in the moment of leadership. In the planning of your words and actions, you will do well to consider not only how you want the others to respond, but also the state you would like them to be left in. Describing this concept in words is difficult. Some metaphors and word pictures that we use are as follows.

You want to speak and act so that the others are left enlivened—more energized.

You want to oxygenate the others; leave them feeling as though they have breathed pure, clean air and feel refreshed and renewed.

You want to have them believe that whatever the situation, they are good people trying to do what works and you support them and want to do whatever you can to resource them. They are not being left alone and isolated. You are with them.

One way to maximize the impact of your leadership is to be thoughtful and active in your planning of the outcomes of your guidance, each time you are going to exercise the Etiquette of Leadership. Envision what will occur once your leadership has been effectively exercised.

This is a creative activity. It will probably not turn out the precise way you envision it; it may not even turn out anything like what you have envisioned. But the purpose of doing this work at this stage is to be thoughtful, creative, playful, considerate and to have an experience. In our experience, a good job done at this stage increases the likelihood that what actually occurs will be more like what you desire than if you had not given the situation any thought at all.

There are lots of types of outcomes; they are more than just what happens. What would you like the outcomes to be?

What are the thinking outcomes that you want from your leadership in the moment? What do you want your followers to be thinking after you have stopped speaking or taking action? Do you want them to be thinking that they can take on what you have asked them to? Do you want them to have made the transition already from wondering whether this is a good thing to do to asking how it can be done? Do you want them to be thinking about the resource implications for themselves and for others? If you do, what do you want them to be left thinking about in each of these areas? Being clear in advance about the specific thinking outcomes you want to leave for others will increase the impact and momentum of your leadership.

There is another outcome you can be thinking about which will also make a significant impact on what you leave behind: how they are connecting, relating and socializing with others. Do you want them to be mingling with one another, talking about what you have said or done in a positive and supportive way? Do you want them to already be modeling in their behaviors the example you have set for them in your leadership intervention, maybe just moments ago? Do you want them to be going back to their desks, thinking about what has been said or done and then communicating with one another in a flurry of emails and tweets? Do you want them to be reviewing what has just happened as they go in small groups for coffee? While you cannot control this, you will do well to give some thought to it in advance so that the quality of your contribution as a leader is maximized.

There is a third outcome: how will each of the people you have spoken to or lead into action feel? What will their individual and collective emotions be? Sad? Purposeful? Elated? Full of trepidation? Angry?

On this latter point, we find that if we plan our leadership intervention and we can foresee emotional responses which do not fit with what we are ethically seeking to accomplish, then it is time to re-plan. Think through again what you are going to do and say in such a way that you can foresee the kinds of emotional responses that you are seeking to achieve for them.

A bonus benefit from preparing in advance what you want to remain after your leadership is that you will sometimes be surprised. Not only could the response of the followers be less than you expected, but it could also be more. No doubt you want your followers to rise to the occasion of leadership. One of the great joys of active leadership occurs in that spontaneous moment when your followers exceed your expectations. But it could also be that they do not respond in the way you have planned.

Either way, this is a moment when the true character and Etiquette of Leadership present themselves in great leaders. You will do well to think about this as being in a dance with yourself. Reflect. Think. Plan.

For us, we have decided that when others do not choose to respond to our leadership in the ways we have planned, and also when they exceed our best expectations, we will seek to be consistent—to continue to set the example. We also have decided that our personal values of integrity and truthfulness will not be sacrificed. We encourage you to think through for yourself how you will respond when those you have sought to lead do not respond to your leadership in a way you have anticipated.

As a practical example, one of us once took on more than we should have in a leadership role; the job was just too big for what we knew we could do in terms of our competency at the time. We decided to share this during a leadership moment with our leadership team. We had planned how we wanted the team to be left after we had said what we were going to say about this. We wanted them to appreciate cognitively that this was a real issue that the team as a whole needed to be aware of. We wanted them to be free to determine for themselves and as a team what they wanted to do next about our overall leadership. And we wanted them to feel positive about the future, while also continuing to feel appreciative of us for dealing with what was an "elephant in the room."

As happens with teams, the responses varied for different team members. At the next gathering of the team a day later, one of the team indicated that she wanted to say something on behalf of the team. She stated that they had all discussed the matter after the last meeting. They all, to a person, had concluded that while one of us was not an ideal leader, we were the best one available. They could see that we were struggling and they wanted to offer their support in moving the project forward. They asked for extra opportunities to provide input and feedback so that we could move our sense of connection to a new level. They said they appreciated that the issue had been raised openly and honestly and that doing it in that way had given them more confidence that the team could work together and that we would achieve the objective.

We were blown away! We told them this and a very open and constructive conversation followed where we determined new ways we could support one another as leader and team members to fulfill the task and to continue to enjoy working together.

Another way this story could have turned out would have been for us to have been met with a coup by our followers; they may have chosen not to continue to be followers.

There is another element of the Etiquette of Leadership that comes into play here; how to apply the Etiquette of Leadership in the face of poor leadership. It might be your poor leadership. It might be poor leadership that occurs in the actions of others. Either way, our experience is that we have a duty as leaders to clean up the mess.

Stop and think—what would you do? What would you choose to leave behind in the aftermath of an experience of poor leadership? This is the place where your real values come alive. Determine what you would say and do in the next interaction you are planning. If it goes wrong, through ineffectual leadership on your part, what will you do? Careful thought and planning in preparation will pay huge dividends. This is like a form of risk management; you may never experience the incident, but planning for how you will treat an event is worth its weight in gold.

If you are exercising the Etiquette of Leadership in your coaching, you will have possibly noticed that this aspect, i.e. what you leave behind or what remains after your leadership, is somewhat akin to one of the layers of coaching that you practice.

In our coaching in the Etiquette of Leadership, we seek to plan coaching conversations that cover five layers—context and concepts, strategies, implementation, immediate next steps, and leverage.

In our experience, the fifth layer of coaching, leverage, often coincides with the question of what remains. It is different in the sense that in coaching, leverage is primarily concerned with how the person being coached can use their new awareness to leverage into other situations in the future. But there is also a sense that what remains after a leadership act creates leverage. We invite you to think also in this space, how will what's left after your action or words of direction create leverage for you and/or for your followers?

Before we leave this section, we need to raise the issue of what happens when you move out of a leadership situation for the last time. What do you leave behind? What remains when you, as a leader, retire, resign, get promoted, die, transfer or move on?

When you exit a leadership situation and are not returning, you will inevitably leave behind some memories, thoughts, and recollections. These are as individual and unique as we each are as human beings. The challenge for you is to practice the Etiquette of Leadership in every command interaction so that some useful aspect of you remains. We might call it your presence. Even though you are now absent, something of you remains. It may or may not be a favorable presence that lingers, and it may linger momentarily or for much longer.

Your presence may remain powerfully for your followership. If you put your hand into a bucket of water and quickly pull it out, the water almost instantly moves to fill the gap occupied by your just-removed hand. Your leadership will leave a longer and more profound gap, directly proportional to the effectiveness of the ways you have exercised the Etiquette of Leadership.

Chapter 12

BRINGING IT ALL TOGETHER

The Etiquette of Leadership does not exist in a vacuum. It has to be practiced with and within our leadership.

In turn, our leadership operates in conjunction with a range of other essential elements in life.

Our approach is that there is a critical relationship that exists between leadership and the living of a good life.

We see that leadership has to be exercised in the context of some work. Work might take many forms and find many expressions. It is essentially a descriptor for all the activities we do in life that require some output and hopefully some positive outcomes.

Our understanding of the Etiquette of Leadership is that leadership works best when it is exercised in the context of some notion of care. A leader using the Etiquette of Leadership will want to operate with the idea that what they are doing or saying as a leader is as a result of their care for a situation or the people involved in it such that they want to make a difference, move things forward or change a situation for the better. We say that none of that caring leadership of activities known as work can effectively be done unless we have a good sense of our own unique identity.

It looks like this.

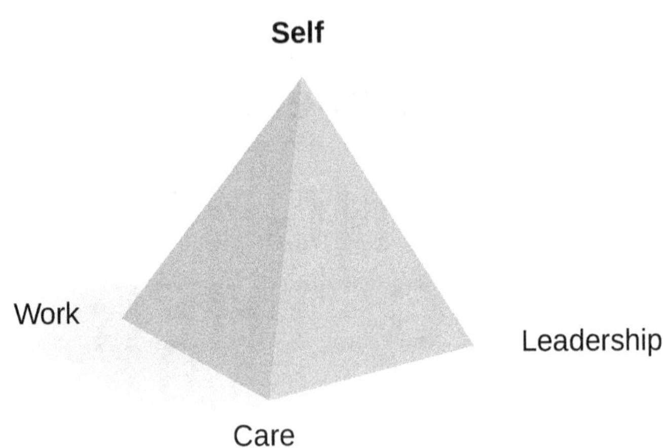

Our experience shows us that as a model this can make a powerful difference in how we lead. When we have a strong identity, when we produce useful action and activity through our work and when we find expression for our deep values through the ways we demonstrate care, we can lead with grace, elegance, and effectiveness.

When we pay attention to the four elements or planes of the triangular pyramid, we can see that we can also find new forms of expression of the Etiquette of Leadership just by paying attention to the interaction between the points on the plane. Let's look at each of these planes and see some examples for each.

When we look at the points of leadership, work, and self, we might see the worth, value and increase in our values that arise from what occurs on that plane.

When we look at the plane that covers work, self, and care, we might see that what we do with a grounded sense of who we are allows us to accomplish otherwise undreamed-of acts of compassion and consider-ateness to one or more others that we lead.

When we look at the plane that covers leadership, work, and care, we might see that through the nature of the work we care currently doing we have an opportunity to increase the capacity of our leadership in a new role that we could take on.

When we look at the plane that covers self, leadership, and care, we might see something like a particular example of some recent acts of leadership that gives us cause to stop and celebrate our accomplishment in that given situation and what it might mean for our future endeavors in similar circumstances.

In addition to examining the interactions between each of the three points on the various planes, it is also possible to look at the interaction between any two points in the triangular pyramid. We suggest you take some time to look at the each of these pairs and think through what the interaction sparks for you and your unique Etiquette of Leadership.

Just to be complete in describing this suggestion further, the interactions are:

- Self and Work

- Self and Care

- Self and Leadership

- Work and Care

- Work and Leadership

- Leadership and Care

Of course, all this exists inside a larger system or ecology of our individual life as a leader and also our life in society as a whole.

In our experience, when the model is being practiced well using the Etiquette of Leadership, we gain a larger and more complete sense of purpose in all these domains of life.

This, in turn, builds awareness and wisdom.

And beyond that is nothingness, eternity or eternal nothingness, depending on your personal philosophy, religion or sense of the ultimate meaning of life.

So, inside an understanding of our life, we come back to the present moment and the next moment that is about to occur after the present moment, where we may choose to exercise leadership utilizing the Etiquette of Leadership. In the present moment or in anticipating the next moment, we get to experience or to begin to create the joy of leadership.

One of the great experiences in life occurs each time we bring together our intention, care, context and models of practice and we speak, or we take a physical step. In that moment, we experience the joy of seeing a creative event occur—someone takes notice or follows. If we had not spoken or acted, that action by another would not have happened. The world would not have been affected the way it will be by what flows from our word or action.

This is the sense of the Etiquette of Leadership being an *art*. All art is creative. In the moment when the painter makes a stroke on the page, when the sculptor touches the clay or stone, when the poet puts the word on paper, or the tattooist applies the needle to the skin, something gets created that would not have existed but for that creative act. So, it is with our words and actions as leaders exercising the Etiquette of Leadership.

The word spoken or the measures taken by us as the leader is like the action of the artist—it produces something. It may or may not be effective in the sense that it is responded to well by the person experiencing it. To the extent that we want to exercise the Etiquette of Leadership well, it will produce a desirable and desired response from our followers.

It is worth repeating what we said just before; if it had not been for our words or actions, the response would not have occurred. It would not have been created in the reaction of another. If it is a significant enough act, it will change the life of the other. It has been brought to life by our leadership and us; by the elegance, grace, and effectiveness of us exercising the Etiquette of Leadership. It would not have existed or have been experienced by the other person except for us speaking or acting. This is creation. This is being creative. This is leadership.

We have created something in the life of another. It can be exhilarating and humbling to have that experience. It can leave you with a deep sense of the joy of leadership; making a difference by your intended, well thought out, caring words or actions that you speak or take in the context you find yourself in that moment of intention.

In that moment of intention, we as effective leaders are seeking to envision success through our leadership. This seems to be a quality shared by all effective leaders, not just those who practice the Etiquette of Leadership. In the lead-up to a leadership act, we are bringing together our sense of the context for the situation requiring leadership. We have a model that guides us in how to think and act; we bring to mind our assurance that we are seeking to exercise leadership because we care for others and we have a clear intention.

In this moment of clarifying our purpose we sometimes will go through a process; we imagine what success through our leadership will look like. Sometimes, if the situation is significant enough, we can even anticipate what our other senses will experience. What will we be hearing ourselves and our followers say? What will we feel if someone touches us? What will we even smell in the moment?

Clarifying our intention in this way is important not only to prepare us for the moment of leadership but also to enable us to imagine creating a shared consciousness for our followers. In the moment when our followers can grasp what we have imagined and own it for themselves, they become enabled. They see that our leadership may result in a possibility being realized or a necessary action taken sufficient for them to give us their trust and confidence.

The non-leader lacks the ability and/or will to do this work in exercising the Etiquette of Leadership. Imagine a situation in your life where leadership will be required in the near future. As an example, imagine you and your team are being confronted by yet another cost reduction exercise at work. You are preparing yourself to apply the Etiquette of Leadership, bringing to mind all you have learned and practiced so far. By contrast, the non-leaders in the team are not doing this work. They are caught up in their own story; they are thinking of ways to avoid, resist or undermine. They just don't care; they are planning how to escape. They believe that by continuing the fantasy of activity for its own sake, they will be okay. They are content to continue on the old path, maybe expecting or merely hoping for a different outcome. Sometimes their resistance will be masked by expressions of care for others, like, "I'm not going along with this because it will do so much harm to others who will be adversely affected. They might lose their jobs or at the least have to do more work and maybe for no increase in pay, so I am not going along with this." In that moment, the non-leadership reveals itself—the non-leader has become trapped.

For us, even paying attention to the reactions of non-leaders in the lead up to our intended leadership act can be invigorating, energizing and instructive. The more we see of their ineffectiveness, the more we can see that our intentions are healthy, generative, creative, enabling, supporting others and building sustainability for the future.

At that moment when we as leaders see the actual and likely responses and even the non-responsiveness of non-leaders, we can feel alone. The strength that can come from that realization, though, is that we see that it is up to us. In that moment, we can come back to our sense of who we are choosing to be in this situation and that will enable us to take the next step or draw in our breath to speak the next word.

When we approach our leadership from this perspective, we soon experience the practical reality that for all our pre-positioning, planning, preparation and anticipation of the moment of leadership, it rarely turns out that way. So, it is with most plans. The value comes from being ready, so that in the response, reaction or reply of the follower that we cannot anticipate, we are then able to adapt and take the next step or say the next useful thing. Each next word or action has the same creative possibility in it. And so, the interaction between leader and follower continues, each interaction being creative, each word spoken or action taken being the source of new words or actions that would not have occurred but for the word or action of you as the leader.

There is another cause for joy in exercising the Etiquette of Leadership, and that is knowing what is occurring in the experience of your followers. Unless you are compelling your followers through an imbalance of power in your favor (e.g. you hold the right to hire and fire, you have a weapon in your hand, you exercise some legislative function that has punitive consequences for non-compliance) the other person or persons will follow you if two conditions are present: trust in you and confidence in the outcome. We mentioned these aspects earlier in Chapter 1 about truth in followership. It is important to reprise this material because this is another point where lots of the ideas of the Etiquette of Leadership come together.

If our followers do not trust us or have confidence in the outcome, it is most likely because they fear something. They may fear our incompetence, or they may fear that the goal is just not possible or whatever. But the result is the same—fear.

In our experience with hundreds of leaders, thousands of conversations and in the practice of tens of thousands of leadership words and actions, we see that fear is the underlying cause of most incompetent leadership. Fear usually generates one of two overwhelming responses—anger or mere compliance.

Mere compliance is so called because if leadership is exercised from a place of power and there is not trust, compliance will occur because there is usually no practical alternative; "If you don't do what I say I will shoot you, prosecute you or sack you." If leadership is not predominantly power driven (but it may be an ingredient) or there is no trust, mere compliance might be expressed as *malicious* compliance. This occurs where the leader does not have the confidence of the follower in them as a leader and/or the follower does not have the confidence in the outcome. Followers will then often maliciously comply so as to do what the leader requires, expecting that it will not produce the leader's desired outcome.

When we exercise the Etiquette of Leadership, we intend it to produce great responses from our followers. In the event that this does not occur and we experience anger or a sense of mere compliance in ourselves or those we are leading, it will most likely be a result of fear. We can usually deal with this effectively by uncovering the source of the fear and dealing with that. When that occurs, creative leadership can resume, using the Etiquette of Leadership.

Having dealt with all this, you can then allow yourself to experience the joy of leadership. It occurs in the moments when everything we have thought about in advance, practiced, experimented with, failed at but chosen to have another go at, finally comes off. We stand. We make a well-timed statement or take well-timed action. We are aware that others are paying attention and they follow where they need to go. It is a sublime moment. This is what a life of leadership feels like.

When we are living as a leader, we are amplifying the joy of life. It is more than our own life. We are experiencing life amplified through, with, as a part of, but not subsumed by the lives of others. We are experiencing what we, ourselves and others, can accomplish when we act together as a result of our leadership.

CONCLUSION

As the nearly 1 billion articles about leadership on the web attest, there is a lot to be said about the subject. Some of it is useful. We hope that The Etiquette of Leadership fits into the useful category for you.

We encourage you to develop your unique Etiquette of Leadership, using the materials here as guides and prompts for your thinking, action, and reflection.

There is both art and science to the Etiquette of Leadership. They unite in our sense of ourselves as leaders as we practice our Etiquette of Leadership through the exercise of our imagination and its progressive contribution in guiding and influencing creative outcomes.

In this sense, being able to exercise the Etiquette of Leadership is a privilege; we are enriched, enlivened and developed every time we practice it.

APPENDIX

> ## HOW TO IDENTIFY AND CONFIRM YOUR UNIQUE LEADERSHIP IDENTITY

*This material is based on The Process Enneagram,
designed by Richard N Knowles.*

As a short refresher about the purpose of this work, you will recall our contention that it is critical to leadership success that we know who we are as a leader and have a clear identity to guide us in our day to day work and life. To the extent that we do that, we will be effective in being able to exercise the Etiquette of Leadership in our everyday acts and our self-leadership.

Many leaders, and indeed just about every one of us humans, go through life with a sense of who we are. It is part of having a healthy personality. Sometimes our sense of identity is clear and well developed; other times it sits in the background of our consciousness. When we deliberately think about who we are, we can recall and describe ourselves, but very often our identity is largely undisclosed.

Our sense of identity is modified by development experiences, reflections, crises and changes in our environment and context, just to name a few.

Many leaders we have worked with have benefitted by making their sense of their identity as leaders explicit. This can be accomplished through experiences like crafted coaching and mentoring, training and self-reflection.

One way we have found that this work can be done involves a process of deliberative inquiry. It can be done alone or in groups. We find that group exploration can be particularly compelling, especially when participants are members of intact teams. However, individual development can also be accomplished.

A way to do this is to engage in a guided development process which is as follows and can be modified in many ways according to need, resources, issues to be addressed, work already done, etc.

For this inquiry, we recommend that you get a good old-fashioned exercise book, a good pen, some blocks of time (initially three one-hour slots in your diary), a quiet place for reflection and inspiration that is free from interruptions, some water for refreshment and a quiet mind.

What follows is a very flexible process. We suggest you roughly follow the stages. You will probably find that as you progress you will get ideas that trigger thoughts about other stages; just highlight them and their relevant stage or draw up your workbook so you can identify which stage they relate to best. For example, in the first stage, "My Current Leadership," you might have a thought about a leadership experience in the past that you would like to use to help you develop further. It may have been a great or a dreadful experience. You might choose to note it down in the Stage 1 notes and/or you may like to add it to your thoughts and ideas about Stage 4.

This is work for you to do on your own, at least initially. It is private to you, although you may choose to engage another person as you work through the process. You may also ultimately opt to share the outcomes of your work more publicly—that is entirely for you to determine.

We suggest you work for about an hour and have a break. Allow your thoughts to develop further and percolate. If further ideas come to mind, have your notes close by and jot down what you are thinking. Be ready for the next time slot you have identified to continue the work.

▶ STAGE 1: MY CURRENT LEADERSHIP

Begin by making notes for yourself about what your ideas of leadership encompass. You might start by using these questions as thought starters:

- *How do I describe my current leadership?*

- *If I was at a job interview and I was asked to say who I am as a leader what would I say?*

- *What is leadership?*

- *How do I define leadership?*

- *How do I distinguish leadership from followership?*

- *What practices and approaches do I notice when someone is leading me?*

- *What models of leadership am I aware of?*

- *Which models do I use or consider useful?*

- *When I think about leaders in my own life, who comes to mind and why?*

- *What particular examples can I recall about times when they lead well or poorly?*

- *What do I feel when I remember those occasions?*

- *Given that reflection, what do I now say leadership is, to me?*

- *How would I describe my leadership to another?*

- *What kind of a leader do I say I am?*

- *What would I say I do now to demonstrate leadership?*

- *What are some examples of recent times when I have shown effective or poor leadership?*

- *Would I say that my leadership is in any way different when I am at work, at home, in community activities, with friends?*

- *If so, how do I see the differences playing out?*

- *What do I notice and recall about times when I have been under stress?*

- *What are some of the roles I fulfill at present that involve the exercise of my leadership?*

- *What accountabilities do I have for leadership?*

- *How do I measure my current effectiveness in leadership?*

- *What instruments or development materials are available to me that indicate my leadership style, strengths, development needs and the like?*

- *What do those materials show?*

- *What do I think about what they say?*

- *Referring back to the material in the book, what are my thoughts about the etiquette of my leadership at present. At what level would I rate my leadership currently?*

- *How do I feel about that?*

▶ STAGE 2: MY LEADERSHIP IN THE FUTURE

- *What kind of a leader would I like to be in the future?*

- *What would I like to be known for as a leader?*

- *What leadership characteristics, activities and behaviors would I like to be practicing in the future?*

- *With whom would I like to be compared favorably as a leader in the future?*

- *Who would I like never to be compared with as a leader in the future?*

- *Why is this?*

- *What could my ultimate leadership level be, referring to the materials in the main book?*

- *What would I like to be doing as a leader in say 5 years' time?*

- *10 years?*

- *25 years?*

- *Who would I like to be leading?*

- *In what roles would I like to be a leader?*

- *What might be my last leadership act before I leave my current position?*

- *What would I like my last leadership act to be before I die?*

- *What would I need to have in place or have accomplished to allow this to occur successfully?*

▶ STAGE 3: MY LEADERSHIP VALUES AND PRINCIPLES

- *What are the important principles and values that I regard as being essential for me as a leader?*

- *What are the top three?*

- *Five?*

- *Ten?*

- *What principles and values would others say I possess?*

- *What do my followers say about my values and principles as a leader?*

- *Which values and principles would I like to develop more capability in as a leader?*

- *What is my weakest value, particularly the one that, if I valued it more, would make a real difference in my leadership?*

- *What examples do I have of my most important values and principles in my leadership?*

- *What short stories can I write down now that illustrate them in action?*

- *What do I do when I find myself confronted by instances where I have not acted consistently with my values and principles?*

- *What responses do I make?*

- *What do I notice is the impact on others when I lead consistently or inconsistently with my values and beliefs?*

▶ STAGE 4: ISSUES AND TENSIONS IN LEADERSHIP

- *Reflecting on the work I have done so far, what comes up for me that I may need to address as issues or tensions in my life as a leader?*

▶ STAGE 5: MY RELATIONSHIPS WITH OTHERS AS A LEADER

- *Who are the people I can identify that are most important to me at the moment in my leadership?*

- *What is the quality of my relationships with them?*

‣ *What might I consider in order to strengthen those relationships?*

‣ *What relationships can I see I need to develop in the future with a view to take my leadership to the next level of effectiveness?*

▶ STAGE 6: THE CONTEXT FOR MY LEADERSHIP AND STRATEGY

‣ *What is going on in the external world to me that might affect my leadership efficacy and growth?*

‣ *What changes do I see that will impact the way I lead, who I lead, the occasions I may have for my leadership to emerge effectively?*

‣ *What is my strategy for my leadership?*

‣ *How could I develop it for the first time or to the next stage of effectiveness?*

‣ *What is my plan to lead others?*

‣ *What does it look like?*

‣ *Is it in written form so I can continue to develop and monitor it?*

▶ STAGE 7: INFORMED LEADERSHIP

‣ *When I think about the people I communicate with about the development of my leadership, who are the most prominent individuals?*

‣ *How do I keep informed about developments leadership understanding?*

‣ *How could I develop information about my leadership?*

‣ *Who are the most influential people who can give me feedback about my direction and build my skills and capability as a leader?*

▶ *As a leader, what are the most efficient ways I share information with others?*

▶ *How do I stay informed as a leader?*

▶ *Rate yourself out of 10 as a listening leader. How could you increase that score?*

▶ STAGE 8: WHAT'S NEXT IN MY LEADERSHIP

▶ *What are the most important tasks for me to take on as a result of this thinking, writing, and reflection?*

▶ STAGE 9: DEEP LEARNING ABOUT MY LEADERSHIP IDENTITY

▶ *Now I have come this far, what have I noticed about my experience of the work I have done?*

▶ *How would I describe my feelings and emotions about this work?*

▶ *Having done this work, what picture do I have of myself now as a leader?*

▶ *What did I notice about myself as I was doing this work?*

▶ *What did I notice about my leadership?*

▶ *What did I notice about what I noticed?*

That completes this part of the work!

Having put this huge amount of great work into the project so far, you could consider what to do next.

Some leaders write it down in a long letter, sometimes addressed to themselves, sometimes to someone they would like to share their work with.

Others write it out as an essay or draw it into a picture to collect the results in the most impactful way for them.

Still, others have written out a statement that captures their thoughts. They then begin to work on expressing their deepened sense of who they are as a leader in the next days and weeks. Whenever they get the opportunity, they reflect on what they have written and often make modifications and additions. In this way, they see this as work in progress, subject to continual development and refinement.

Yet another way you might use the work you have done is to craft it into a form you are happy enough with to share with another person you have confidence in. You might consider doing something like reading the work out and asking for their feedback and comments. A particularly useful way to get feedback is to ask them to make their responses in the form of, "Would you consider X?" "Would you consider Y?

Whichever you choose, we wish you all the best in your leadership and the ways it shows up in the Etiquette of your Leadership!